OPEN TO THE INFINITE RICHES OF THE UNIVERSE

AND LIVE A BALANCED LIFE FULL OF MIRACLES, WEALTH, ABUNDANCE, BLISS, AND TRIUMPH

OPEN TO THE INFINITE RICHES OF THE UNIVERSE

AND LIVE A BALANCED LIFE FULL OF MIRACLES, WEALTH, ABUNDANCE, BLISS, AND TRIUMPH

BY

ZOEY ZLATOSLAVA PETRAK

www.StrategicResultsMentor.com

Published by
Golden Glory Publishing
Ontario, Canada

ISBN 978-1-61863-631-7

Library of Congress Control Number: 2013920970

DISCLAIMER

The author of this book does not give financial or medical advice or
prescribe any technique as a treatment for financial, physical, emotional
or medical problems. The information contained in this book is an
opinion, and no part of this book is to be considered financial, medical,
legal, or personal advice. This publication is intended only to offer
information of a general nature in order to help people in their search
for happiness, and emotional and spiritual wellbeing. The advice and
strategies contained in this book may not be suitable for your particular
situation. All readers should consult with a professional where
appropriate. Not all systems work for all people. In case you use any
information from this book, the author and the publisher assume no
responsibility for your actions. Neither the author nor the publisher
shall be liable for any loss or any other damages resulting from said
use.

Printed in the United States of America

CONTENTS

I

INTRODUCTION

Hello, my dear reader. In *OPEN TO THE INFINITE RICHES OF THE UNIVERSE*, I would like to talk about an important topic that we have to take care of every day. I would like to talk about wealth and abundance. You would agree with me that in our society monetary issues are pretty important. No matter whether a person is from the middle class, or is poor, or is rich, every person has to deal with financial matters every day, whether he or she wants to or not. That's life. Even if the person thinks that money is the root of all evil, whether the person loves or hates money, he still has to think and deal with money every day for the rest of his life.

This issue can sometimes be very complicated, and even painful if you always have to struggle to make ends meet. And even if you are not desperate, you still might not have enough funds to fulfill your biggest dreams, or maybe even the smallest. So you see that money is an important issue, whether you want it to be important or not.

People work a lot to support themselves and their families; and very often they work at jobs they don't like or are not happy with, and jobs that don't pay much. They spend more time working than they do anything else in their lives, when for many of them work is not even their priority. They think that their priority is their kids, and families; and maybe they have some desire to travel or to buy a nice gift for someone they love, or to buy a house. All of these things are important to us and we think that they are our priorities. We think that our goal and priority is to provide a happy, joyous and prosperous life for ourselves and for people we love, but as a result many people spend almost all their time doing something that is not really their main priority. They do this just to make some little money to pay for the food and rent, and this goes on month after month and year after year; and many generations spend their entire lives running in this never-ending circle and never feeling happy or satisfied. Does this make any sense: "I want this, but in order to have this I will do something else and will never even have time to do what I really desire?"

Many people don't even think about this pattern, and some people try not to think about it. Many feel powerless, and they are sure that they cannot change anything, that their lives are meant to be this way. And many feel constant fear over their financial future. They fight with their spouses, friends, and people they love. Many families fall apart because people cannot handle the pressure of financial instability and the constant lack of everything. They become angry, unsatisfied, miserable and hurt. They see no way out of this situation. Sometimes they don't even realized what's wrong. They try not to think about what's going on and they never look for any solutions. Some of them even turn to alcohol and bad habits to forget about their harsh reality and their constant dissatisfaction. Many people are sure that they are powerless and cannot do anything about it, and so they just accept the reality and struggle.

They don't even realize that they limit themselves with these beliefs, and that no one else can limit them except themselves. And very often it's not just money they feel the lack of. In order to be truly abundant, a person should be wealthy and satisfied in all aspects of his or her life; the person should be balanced in his abundance. It is important to understand this because there are people who can be called successful, and even rich, but whose personal happiness is not on the same level as their success and wealth. True abundance is when you feel the constant flow of love, freedom, health, happiness and wealth in all aspects of your life; and no one can limit us except ourselves. We are the creators of our destiny and our experiences, and something within us makes us experience what we experience today.

If you realize that your financial situation is not what you desire it to be, if you are tired of constant struggles to make ends meet, if you are tired of debts and fear about your future finances, if you really want to change this situation, if you really are tired of poverty and lack, then you can change all this. If you want to be successful, feel and be wealthy, happy and abundant, you really can do it, because one of the most important things to implement the necessary changes is to understand and realize your problem and make a decision.

You should see clearly what you don't want and decide what you do want. And also you should always know that you do have the power within you to change your financial situation and to create miracles in all aspects of your life. You are not alone; the Almighty Infinite Intelligence created you and will always help you and lead you to the best outcome possible. You should always listen to this eternal wisdom within you, for it will show you the way. It will open the doors for you.

> *"Ask, and it will be given you; search, and you will find; knock, and the door will be opened for you. For everyone who asks receives, and everyone who searches finds, and for everyone who knocks, the door will be opened."* (Matthew 7:7-8)

You see, because you are holding this book right now, it means that you are looking for the answer. Follow your heart and you will find it with the help of the One who is always by your side.

This book is designed for us to see and open ourselves to the Infinite Riches that the Universe always has for us and always gives us in unlimited quantity every second, and to allow ourselves to enjoy these riches in all aspects of our lives forever and always. We live in the perfect and abundant Universe. We are created perfect; and we live in the perfect world that was created especially for us. Therefore we deserve the best, we deserve happiness, we deserve wealth and abundance. It is our right, which was given to us as a gift at birth. We have all the riches of the Universe at our doorstep; everywhere we look, it surrounds us. Look at the oceans, the magnificent mountains, the snow, the sun, the birds, the rain, the flowers, the forests, the jungles, and the animals. Look at the clouds, the planets, and the stars in the sky. Look at the light, the darkness, the fields, the air, the grass. These are all amazing miracles that we have grown accustomed to and thus don't pay much attention to — but they are all here, and they are all here for us. It is all our abundance, it is all our world given to us as a gift. We are so abundant that we can't even imagine the boundaries of our abundance.

You should also remember that we are parts of the Whole, and that there is a part of the Divine in each and every one of us. You already are abundant; there is no other way, it just does not exist. All we have to do is to open ourselves, open and accept these treasures that are surrounding us and telling us to take them and to use as much as we need and can. And there will never be an end to it, because the Universe is infinite, and the Power that governs everything is Eternal and Almighty.

But you are always given a choice. The Divine loves you, and you are free to choose, you are free to choose what you want to experience here on this planet. And if you realize it, understand what you don't want to experience and what you do want and desire to experience, then you can make a choice. You can decide to open yourself to success, beauty, happiness, wealth, abundance and triumph in this life. All of these treasures already surround you; you just have to make a choice, decide what you want and open yourself to the Infinite Riches that the Universe has for you and experience it, live it here and now.

You should always listen to your inner feelings, determine what's right for you, and trust yourself and the Divine who is leading you. Now you are more than ready to begin this journey.

Enjoy the book, explore the possibilities, and live your dreams.

II

REALIZE YOUR DESIRE

F irst of all, it is important to know what you really want. You have to be clear and understand your desires, your goals. Dreams and desires move us, make us improve; they push us to reach and achieve new heights. Therefore, if the dreams are sincere and if they are good in their nature and intention, they are your blessings, they show you the way, they help you and motivate you to reach the highest of your potential, to open up your talents and realize your hidden gifts. That's why if you have a dream it is meant to come true, if you let it, if you allow yourself to live your dream and open yourself to the blessings of the Universe.

So, understand your desire and state it. It is important to be specific, to be exact, to know exactly what you want, and to really want it. So pay attention to your desire and focus on it. Maybe you want to be financially free, wealthy, or be abundant in all aspects of your life, or to be happy. You have to make sure that you know what you want and know that you really want it, and that you want exactly this. That's a first step.

If we are talking about the financial situation of a person, for the riches to flow into a person's life, it is important to find your right place in life. You see, our Universe is harmony, love, and balance. So everything has to be balanced. If you hate your job, if you hate every moment you spend there, if you are not happy, if you are miserable and depressed, then you can't expect that job to bring you abundance. If you think about it, it just does not make any sense.

There are many people who truly don't know what they like or enjoy doing as their profession. Maybe, when they were kids, they had some fantasies such as becoming a famous actor, singer, or musician, but when they grew up they could not make up their mind on what they should do.

So, they just went to college or University and studied what their parents told them to study, or maybe what they figured would bring them a good income, or they just picked anything that sounded good in the course description. And that's how they arrived at their profession.

Some of them were lucky, and maybe they were able to find a good job, which they truly liked. So, their accidental choice was actually right for them. But others soon understood that they couldn't find a decent job; or, even if they did, they somehow are not so happy doing what they are doing. Some people never even think about this. They got the job, they wake up every day with the alarm clock, they come to work, and they feel annoyed and hate-filled because of it. They go to work and wait until Friday comes, and are really sad when it is Sunday night again. But they don't think about it. They just know — it's life. They just say to themselves: "That's what I have to do every day. That's all." There are many such people who change their careers once, twice, or even more. Sometimes it helps, but sometimes it does not. Sometimes people can never understand what they are good at, or what they would enjoy doing. At least that's how it seems to them.

So, if you have a job that you are not happy with, it doesn't necessarily have to mean that now you have to quit it and find something else, who knows what. Instead, you should try to listen to yourself and feel what is right for you; maybe you are already at your perfect place, but maybe you just don't realize it. Maybe you have to change your attitude towards your job, your tasks, your colleagues, and your whole work situation, and in many cases this will be more than enough. Try to feel love towards your job, your profession, your environment; try to feel gratitude towards the people you work with, the tasks you have to do every day, and even the traffic on your way home. This might just be enough for you to really appreciate what you are doing and start enjoying it to the fullest.

But perhaps some people cannot open up to their fullest potential doing what they are doing right now; sometimes this can be the case. We spend a lot of time at work; I would say most of our day, every day. And it is really important to be at the right place, to be doing the best that you can, to enjoy it to the fullest, to open up all your talents, and to be really and truly successful. When you are at the right place, you help yourself to become the professional you want to be and help the others by delivering the best service possible, because you are the best person for this job; you love it and really enjoy it. And the Universe will respond to your feelings of joy and satisfaction by sending you a great flow of income, which will pay you for your talents and amazing work.

There also are people who have lost a job and can't find a decent one. There are people who were never able to find a decent job, and who work at low-paid places. There are people who don't have enough education, or don't have any education at all, and blame their lack of education for all their struggles.

It does not matter if you are young or old, if you are educated or have no education, if you are rich or poor, if you have a job or never had a good one, or if you cannot find one. What is important, always, is to love what you are doing and to find your place in life.

All of us are different. We have different goals, desires, and talents, different wishes, and different understandings of financial wellbeing, and this is great. The diversity is amazing; it is the beauty of ever-changing life. It is great that we are all different. If we all fulfill our career dreams, it does not mean that everyone will want to become a banker or a pilot, or a housewife. We all have different desires, and we all have different understandings of achievement, success, and triumph. And this is amazing.

Some people dream of becoming lawyers, while others dream of becoming doctors, cashiers, business owners, hairdressers, or drivers. You see, if you become a nurse, or a janitor, or a pilot, or a builder, etc., you might not be very happy and willing to work at these jobs, but there are people who would be genuinely happy doing this kind of work and would really enjoy it. Likewise, maybe your friend would not enjoy doing what you like to do. Some people want to be really wealthy and become a CEO of a great corporation, but others want to enjoy the quiet life, living in a quiet, small house near the sea. Still others would love to have an apartment downtown, while their friends would enjoy living on a yacht. These differences are why this world is so diverse and beautiful.

If everyone finds their true place, people will be happier and wealthier, because if you are happy and joyous all other good things will just follow. And we will have enough people working and serving at their best potential in every possible job position. So, it is really important to find your true place in life.

You should always be thankful for your current and past experiences, even if they are not what you think you want them to be. Because, first of all, they did help you understand what you don't want to do, and what you do want to do, in your life; or at least they made you search for the answer. And secondly, they all prepared you in their own ways for your future success. They all led you through different stages, which helped you become the way you are today. So, you should always be thankful for what you had and what you have. You should feel love, gratitude, and joy towards the things you do, experience, and have.

However, there is nothing static in this world. Therefore, things that are ideal for you today might change, and might not seem so perfect and ideal to you in the future. This can happen with a job or a business that supports you. So, it is important for you to find your best place for this specific time, and to truly enjoy what you are doing.

Here are some affirmations that have helped and still help me find the true place in my life:

"Thank You God for helping me find my true place in life. Thank You for showing me the best way for me. Thank You for opening my real, genuine talents, and thank You for showing me my Divine true purpose. Thank You God for this gift. Thank You for the work or business that I truly love. Thank You that I already have my ideal work/business. This work/business brings me great profit and a lot of money. It brings me satisfaction, joy, success, happiness, calmness, free time and wealth. Thank You that I already have my successful career. Thank You that I am successful, wealthy, calm, and relaxed. Thank You for my beautiful, easy, happy, healthy, abundant, interesting life, full of love, gratitude and happiness. Thank You that I am healthy, satisfied, calm, successful, abundant, wealthy, and happy! Thank You for a lot of free time, which I can spend and enjoy with my family and people

I love. Thank You for Your Divine gifts and blessings that You are sending my way! Thank You for Your love and protection. Thank You!

"Thank You God that You always tell what is perfect and right for me. Thank You for showing me the right decisions, and that I always know what I want and what is right and what is best to do. Thank You God for Your love, Your guidance, Your wisdom, Your calmness, Your peace, Your love, and Your protection! I love You!

"Thank You God for the right and the best decision for me and for everybody! Thank You God for Your eternal wisdom, for You leading me to what is perfect and right for me. Thank You for Your guidance, Your blessings, Your love, and Your protection. Thank You God for the fastest and the best answers, and for the best results possible! Thank You!

"I am in my right place, I am happy, I am successful, I am wealthy, I am prosperous, I am calm, and I am happy. I feel love and I am loved! Thank You!"

You can add more affirmations of your own by saying: "*I am...*" and continue with positive things you want to become.

You can read these affirmations in the morning or in the evening, before going to bed, or maybe even three times a day. You can change them or add things that you feel should be there specifically for you. You should always listen to your inner voice, which tells you what is right and how to do it best. No one knows better than your inner self. Therefore, trust yourself, listen to your heart, and follow the inner wisdom in you. Let the Divine lead you to your perfect place in life, where you will be genuinely happy, successful, and satisfied.

III

CLEAR NEGATIVE BELIEFS FROM YOUR PATH

Another important step on the road to wealth and success is to change, and let go of your negative beliefs towards money, wealth, wealthy people, abundance, and the wealthy lifestyle. Most of us have at least a few negative ideas about money. Sometimes it is really difficult to say whether you do have them or not, because they can be hidden deep in your subconsciousness. Maybe you heard something negative about wealth in the past, maybe even in your childhood, from your parents, relatives, neighbors, or friends. Maybe you believed in some false prejudices, some incorrect interpretation of universal laws — who knows?

We have all heard many different negative ideas about money, such that as money is dirty and the root of all evil, that poverty is the road to enlightenment, that money changes people, that rich people are greedy — and all sorts of other popular beliefs about money and wealth. If you do have any such negative beliefs towards money, whether you realize you have them or not, these beliefs will block you and protect you from the "evil" that is money — which will block the free flow of money into your life. If you believe that money is evil, then you will protect yourself from it on a subconscious level.

Let's just think for a second about all those negative beliefs that people like to feed one another about money and wealth. Money is not good or bad; it is just paper, a means of exchange. In the past, people traded cows or potatoes for bread and milk. So did this make cows or potatoes bad or evil? Money is simply currency that we use to exchange for different goods or services. Again, money cannot be good or bad; it is just paper.

Therefore, this paper called money cannot make its owner bad or good just because he has it. The money does not change the person, does not make him bad; the person just has more opportunity and freedom to show his real nature and his real character when he becomes more powerful and rich. If the person possesses a good nature, when he becomes rich he will have more opportunities to perform good deeds. He will help others, organize charities, and build hospitals. Or maybe the person will decide to help only his parents, friends, relatives, and kids — or maybe just to make his own life happier. Even if the latter is the case, as a result we will have one more happy person on our planet, which is amazing!

If the person is greedy, if he shows negative character traits and acts like a snob, it's not because the money changed him; it happened because he was always like this, but now with more money he has more chances to show his negative traits. That's all. So, it is not money that makes us bad or good. It is us and our conscious choices.

16

Therefore you have to realize that those negative beliefs about money and wealth are not true. They are false, and you should let go of them. Get rid of them. Clear your path and welcome the wisdom of the Universe which is in you. You just have to remind yourself about it, and this wisdom will come forth. It is always with us all; we just often pretend to forget about it and pretend that we never knew about it. But as soon as you remind yourself and open up to the Divine Wisdom that is in each and every one of us, you will know, you will follow your heart, and you will feel what is right for you. Remember, no one knows what is right for you better than you do when you surrender and let the Divine Wisdom within you lead you to the perfect destination, to your dreams, to the life you desire and deserve.

The following affirmation can help you to relax, trust, let go of your negativity, and open yourself to the riches that are given to us all the time:

"Thank You God for the infinite riches You send my way. Thank You for Your love, peace, protection, and happiness. Thank You for Your generous gifts, which fill all aspects of my life. Thank You for my having accepted Your blessings with love and gratitude. I am happy, healthy, and wealthy; I am prosperous, successful, abundant, and grateful. I am filled with love and gratitude. Thank You."

The negative beliefs about money and wealth can have different forms. Some people don't have any negativity towards money or wealth, or they already worked on and got rid of that negativity; but they might be afraid that something could happen to them if they receive news that is too good. They are afraid that they won't be able to handle the shock of the happy news, that it might be too much for them to handle. This kind of fear might appear when the person gets too close to the fulfillment of a really big dream very fast. Some people are afraid that if they become really successful, everyone will envy them, and that the result will be an atmosphere that will not be very friendly towards them. Others feel that if they get something they want, they might lose it. Someone could take it away from them, or steal it; someone could sue them. Some people are afraid that they are going to lose their friends, and the familiar lifestyle they have today which is already very comfortable for them. Maybe they are even afraid that they might lose their spouse, who would not want to change to a different lifestyle.

From one side these arguments might look really silly, because usually the person wants these changes to occur, but on the other hand, somewhere deep inside, he or she might have these hidden fears that don't reveal themselves so easily. These kinds of fears can also block a person from achieving his or her dreams and goals. These fears are acting as blocks that try to "protect" you from undesired outcomes by not letting you get there in the first place. Pretty logical, right?

Again, if you stop and examine these fears more closely, you will realize that they are not legitimate, they are not real. They are just the opposite of what you desire. Therefore, you don't need them. You don't need these false negative beliefs. So just get rid of them. It's that easy!

Always remember, always know, that you are the creation of the Divine, that His wisdom and love are within you. He always blesses you, leads and directs you to whatever is perfect and right for you. You will always remain yourself, whether rich or poor, if you so choose. You have the power to make choices, and to be the person you choose to be in any circumstances. Therefore, if you choose wealth to highlight all you best qualities and will live by the rule, *"Do to others as you would have them do to you"* (Matthew 7:12), God's blessings will materialize through you.

You should also remember that God would never send anything that you cannot handle. He knows you. He created you. He knows what's best for you. So trust Him and let go. Release yourself from these fetters that try to hold you back from where you belong and from achieving your highest goals and reaching your highest potential. These fetters are not real, so they cannot hold you for long. But why wait any longer? You can do it now!

IV

FEELING IS THE KEY FACTOR

Our creation process starts with our thinking and feeling. Whatever we focus our thoughts on during the day, whatever we think about, we bring into our life, we attract it. The brilliant thing about this process is that we have a choice, we are given this choice: We can choose what we want and what we don't want to bring into our lives. We can choose what to think about and how to feel about it. By disciplining our thoughts and feelings, we can manifest what we desire, and enjoy the life of our dreams, as soon as we understand this principle and master it. Let's talk about feelings.

Feelings are a very important part of the manifestation process. Our Universe is the feeling Universe, and we have feelings for a reason. Therefore, feelings play a crucial role in the creation process. Knowing what you want and simply stating it is not enough. You have to have the corresponding feeling. Saying and thinking "I am wealthy" is a good first step towards your goal, but it is not enough; you have to feel it! We attract what we feel throughout the day, and it materializes in our lives, and then we ask ourselves interesting questions: "Why did this happen to me?" "What did I do to bring this into my life?" "Why? Why?"

Our feelings come from our thoughts. We think something and then we feel either bad or good depending on our thought, and we attract what we feel and think about. In order to achieve our goals and live the life we desire, we have to discipline our thinking, discipline what we picture in our mind and discipline our imagination. It is difficult to control our thoughts; therefore, we have to pay attention to what and how we feel. Feelings are good indicators; they show us if we focus on something we want or on something we don't want. It is pretty easy: If you feel good, you think about what you want and you create it; and if you feel bad, you create the opposite of what you want, which is why you feel bad.

So, in order to achieve your goals and to manifest what you desire, you should focus your thoughts on those goals and what you desire. Think about them as if you have already achieved them. Picture yourself enjoying every moment because you have already received what you want. So, what you think about and what you concentrate all your attention on, you will attract to your life. When you are focusing your thoughts on your desires, when you are visualizing or imagining the desired outcome, it is also important to focus on gratitude for the answered prayer, to focus on already having what you asked for.

Very often people start thinking about things that they want; but instead of focusing on pleasant thoughts of having already achieved their goal, they often focus on lacking the things they want. So, if you think about things that you desire, like wealth, a good job, a new car, a soul mate or a spouse, and you feel bad, that means you are focusing on not having what you want. You start getting nervous and worried. Questions like "When and how am I going to get it?" and "Why it is not in my life yet?" start to pop up in your head, and you start feeling bad. The bad feeling is the indicator which shows you that you are not focusing on and attracting what you want, but instead are actually focusing on the lack of what you want. That's why you feel bad. So, watch your feelings, and change your thoughts from ones about lack to thoughts about gratitude, receiving, and already heaving what you want.

So stating your goal and disciplining your thinking and imagination to focus on what you desire are crucial; but it is also very important to feel what you want to create. Feel the joy, feel that you already have what you are asking for. Live your dream now. You don't have to wait until it materializes to enjoy this moment; do it now. For example, if you want to have a house, imagine how you would feel living in that house. Imagine what kind of feelings you would have opening the door of that house, going up the stairs, and living there. Focus on the feelings. It is much better than to just say, "I want this particular house. I need only this house and no other house. This is the house of my dreams and I will be happy here."

What you might not know is that it might not be the best house for you; maybe there is another much-better house, a house that is made just for you, and which is beyond any of your current dreams.

You might not know this, but God knows everything. He always knows what is best for you. Be flexible; let the Universe bring you what is perfect and right for you, according to your feelings. So, instead of focusing on the specific object and demanding it, it is much better to feel the feelings you want to have when you already own the house of your dreams, and let the Universe choose the perfect house for you. This is because sometimes you might not hear and realize what you really want, because you want it so much. The feelings that you send to the Universe will materialize your desire in the perfect form. That's why many people sometimes experience outcomes better than they could ever imagine. They had the feeling, and the Universe did everything to fulfill it.

So feel the way you want, feel like you've already achieved what you desire. If you want to be wealthy, feel wealthy, feel it right now. It is like a game. You remember how, when you were a kid and were playing with toys, you could pretend to be whatever you wanted — a doctor, a teacher, a pilot, a king, or Cinderella. It was easy then. But you can still play a similar game, through your feelings, now. It does not mean you have to do anything strange physically. Don't go and spend a fortune on something, or do anything stupid. You don't have to actually do anything, just engage your feelings. No matter what you have in your life right now, know and feel that you are a wealthy person. God's child cannot be poor; this is an illusion, which was created by your earlier feelings which did not support your goals.

There is part of the Divine in you; there is God's power in you. God is always with you. He always helps you. He can never fail. You can never fail! Feel that you have already achieved what you want. Feel that you are living the life of your dreams. Feel this calm, sure feeling of peace, calmness, and quiet happiness arising from the answered prayer. Put yourself in the state of feeling and living the life you desire and deserve. Live with this feeling, wake up with this feeling, go to work feeling your wealth and worthiness. Feel it throughout the day and before going to bed at night. Feel it in you, in your every word, your every movement, and your every thought. You already have it. *"Before they call I will answer, while they are yet speaking I will hear."* (Isaiah 65:24)

It is difficult to describe with words. That's why many books write about it but not everyone can put into practice and apply it right away. But in reality it is much easier than anyone can explain or write about it. Just imagine explaining to someone how to write: "You take the pen, and put it on the paper and hold it with your fingers and …"; or explaining how to eat, or what something tastes like. In reality feeling is much easier and natural than written explanation.

So pretend — like you pretended to be a king or a princess when you were a kid. Again, it is not about what you do, it is about how you feel. So feel wealthy right here and now, right at this very moment. And really, you don't even have to be pretending, because everything you want, everything all of us want, already exists, and you already are everything that you've ever wanted to be, because you are God's child. Part of the Divine, with its wisdom, strength, and power, is within you. So you already are wealthy. You just need to open yourself to this realization, and the actual materialization of what you want will not make you wait for long.

Make sure you are not too hard on yourself and your goals. If you want to achieve something, if you are working on achieving your goal, the feeling of ease is also significant. When you feel desperate, when you don't know what else you can do to finally make this process work, when your calmness and happiness depend on the outcome, when you feel that you need it, you need it right now, when you are too much into the thing you desire, you are not at ease anymore. Your heart belongs to it in an "unhealthy way," and you are desperate and needy. Your mood depends on whether you get it. If you feel that, you have to stop, because at this point you are focusing on actually not having the thing that you want, then you are focusing on lack.

Think about this: How can you be desperate if you already have it? How can you be needy if your prayer has already been answered? How can you feel upset, with your happiness depending on the outcome, if you already know and have achieved the desired outcome? How can you not feel ease if everything is already here for you? Everything you could ever need or want is already here, like apples in the apple orchard; your riches are plentiful and just sitting there waiting for you!

Therefore, decide what you want, state your goal, think about it as you already have it, be grateful, and let go of it. Let the Divine bring everything you need into your life. It is already there. Just open yourself with ease and accept these unlimited riches that the Universe offers to every one of us all the time. Let go of desperate feelings, of any kind of need, and even of your desire. Know that the Divine Wisdom in you leads you to whatever is perfect for you. God is always by your side, He guides you. The Divine knows exactly what you are looking for, and knows what exactly is perfect and right for you. Let go, trust and receive with ease all the riches which are already yours, which are created for you, and which are now materializing into your existence.

Let go. Feel calm and relaxed. Trust God, His unlimited and unconditional love, and His wisdom, and enjoy His generous gifts, His abundance, His wealth, and His bliss, which are already here, all around you. They are already yours. Just open yourself to them and let yourself live the life you desire and deserve. God loves you. He wants you to be happy. You are His beloved child. He is always by your side. He is closer than you think He is. You can relax, trust, and let go. Let the Divine lead you. And watch the Universe uncover your treasures right before your eyes.

V

PROGRAMMING THE SUBCONSCIOUSNESS TO ACHIEVE UNLIMITED SUCCESS AND INFINITE RICHES

As we've already talked about, disciplined thinking and disciplined imagination play crucial roles in the creation process. The way we think, the things we believe in, and the patterns of our behavior are determined by our inner beliefs, and by our perception of the world, of life, of the laws governing the world and life, and of ourselves. Our subconscious mind has been programmed since our childhood. The information that we hear every day, the beliefs of our parents, the things that our society dictates, the things that we see around us every day, impact our inner beliefs and leave their imprint in our subconsciousness. These beliefs, very often, are responsible for the results that we get, for the level of success and satisfaction that we have, and for many other factors that we experience in life. Sometimes our beliefs help us, but sometimes they act as blocks that prevent us from getting what we want.

Our subconscious mind can be programmed, and it responds to suggestions; it's all natural. That's how we got

29

our beliefs in the first place. Maybe you heard something your father said when you were a child, something like, "Money doesn't grow on trees," and you believed that statement. You accepted it to be your truth, and it has stayed with you as if programmed into you, as your rule and your law.

So, if your subconscious mind responds to suggestions, it can be reprogrammed. You can realize, you can understand, that what you have believed in, starting a long time ago, is simply false, is not true. It was your false belief.

But when you learn the laws of the Universe, show yourself the true laws, teach yourself, acquire new beliefs, and educate yourself, you can exchange those blocks with things that will actually help you in achieving your goals.

For example, many centuries ago people believed that the Earth was flat. This was a false belief. No matter what they thought, however, the Earth has always been round. Over time, explorers and scientists learned the truth of this, and people changed and rejected their flat-earth belief. This realization of the truth actually served humanity and opened the door to many other new discoveries. Would it be helpful if people continued to be stubborn and still believed in something that is not true and in something that blocks them from new discoveries, development, and evolution?

Whatever you believe in, you will attract and create it for yourself. That's why different people might have different results doing the same thing. They attract what they believe is true for them.

For example, two friends studied together to get a good profession; they wanted to become lawyers. They had the same education, the same funds, even earned the same grades in law school, and the same capital to start a legal practice business. Nevertheless, one is a successful and famous lawyer, while the other has many debts and is struggling to make ends meet. This is because their beliefs were very different, positive versus negative, and they thus attained (attracted) different results.

It is not that easy to start, to all of a sudden think and feel in a different direction, if you have been thinking in the opposite way your whole life. Your habits and inner beliefs will dictate your behavior, but it is possible to make these changes. Again, you have a choice, and this choice you make with your conscious mind. You can educate yourself and reprogram your inner beliefs and your subconscious mind by disciplining your thinking process; you make a conscious choice, work on it, and stay loyal to achieving your goals. Affirmations are very helpful in this process.

In order to discipline our thinking and to focus on the thoughts that can help us materialize our goals, we have to consciously choose and lead our thought process until this new positive thinking process will take on a life of its own and become automatic. By repeating affirmations, phrases, and prayers, we can make ourselves, our subconscious mind, accept things that we affirm — these positive new beliefs as true for us. Focusing our thoughts throughout the day on what we want will help us to attract it and materialize it in our life.

To help yourself in this process, you can read affirmations a few times a day. You can start at three times a day — the first time in the morning, when you wake up; the second in the afternoon; and the third in the evening before you go to bed. If you feel you need to do this more than three times per day, if you feel that three times is not enough, or when you do it and you start thinking that it does not work, repeat these affirmations more often. You can do it seven or more times a day, throughout the day, for about 10 to 15 minutes each time, for a week or two, or as long as you need to make yourself accept the affirmations as true for yourself, until you feel the calmness, satisfaction, gratitude, and happy expectation of the answered prayer.

Some people tried reading and repeating affirmations in the past. Sometimes people do it, and over time they see no changes, so they give up, saying something like, "It doesn't work" or "It doesn't work for me." And they stop, even before the results start appearing, not even giving the results a chance to appear in their lives.

But think about this: The Power of God is always with you. The part of the Divine is in you. God's wisdom, His power, His love, and His support are within you; they surround you. How can something not work for God? How can God fail? How can His power be not enough to achieve anything? *"For God all things are possible."* (Matthew 19:26)

Just give these truths that you affirm a chance to take root in your subconsciousness, and give them time to show their treasures.

If it is 3:00 in the morning, you know that the sun will rise within a few hours. It does not matter that you cannot see it at 3:00 a.m. You know that at 5:00 or 6:00 a.m. the sun will rise; you know that it is already there, in the sky. When the time comes, it will wake the world up in the glory of its light and warmth. Allow the riches of the Universe to root within you, and have enough patience so that it can unfold in your life in its unlimited glory, and bring you the treasures that you deserve.

It is also really important to actually do it, to actually go through this process of reading the affirmations. Some people have heard about affirmations many times, having read about different affirmations in different books, but they never had enough motivations to actually try affirmations, or to do so for as long as it takes to see the results. Saying, "Yeah, Yeah, but it does not work," when you have never really tried affirmations does not help you at all.

How tired are you from not achieving what you want? How tired are you from leaving your dreams for later? If you decide right now that you do want the changes in your life, if you really want these changes to take place, if you want it so badly that you can invest your time and attention to it, just do it. Read the affirmations and see for yourself.

When you affirm Divine Truths, when your goal is based on love and wellbeing for everyone, when you are sincere and focused, when you are thankful, and when you live by the rule *"Do to others as you would have them do to you"* (Matthew 7:12), Divine blessings are with you. When you read the affirmations during the day for five, 10, or 15 minutes, they will help you stay focused on your goals and they will discipline your thought process. They will keep you thinking about what you want, throughout the day. They will also discipline your feelings, because our thoughts influence our feelings. And, as you already know, what you think about throughout the day you attract.

This is a really easy way that can help you focus your thoughts, and discipline the thinking and feeling process the way you want. The Divine Truths that you affirm will sink into your subconscious mind over time. This way, you can change the false beliefs that do not serve you and remove the blocks that prevent you from achieving what you want. At the same time, you will sow the beliefs that will help you reap the rich harvest, because when you are ready, you will see the sprouts of your efforts growing in the fields of your mind and life.

You can find affirmations in different books, or you can write them yourself, or create a mix of your own affirmations and affirmations already offered by different authors. It is a good idea to add something to someone else's affirmations, edit them or create your own, because you know yourself better than anybody else. You know what you want, you know your feelings and your thoughts, you know your goals. Listen to yourself, find your own words that can describe what you want, words that can touch your feelings and put you in a positive mood. Listen to the infinite wisdom of the Divine in you. Ask God to lead you and direct you, and write your own affirmations or add to existing ones.

You can write one affirmation today, read it for a few days, and if you feel you need to expand upon it, you can write a new one or add something else to the existing one. Sometimes, when you read your affirmations, all of a sudden you can start feeling that you also have to work on some specific aspect of your life, such as your relationships, your career, your business, or something else. You might feel that you also worry about something else, or that there is something you are not very satisfied with in your life. Just write an affirmation on that issue. It can be a few words, or a sentence, or a paragraph, or even a few pages in length. If you want to read affirmations written by others, choose to read only those affirmations that you feel are right for you, that make you feel good and that work on the issues that you want to improve in your life.

It is better to actually write affirmations on paper by hand than to type them. It can also be a good idea to actually handwrite an affirmation even if you found it in a book. When you affirm something, when you read affirmations, try to feel the words and ideas mentioned in them. Try to understand, think, and feel those words and ideas, and do it with feeling. Feelings are the fuel that makes affirmations work. Believe in what you affirm. Believe that your prayer will be answered. Believe that God wants the best for you, that He loves and supports you.

Our desires and our dreams move us forward, make us act and grow. We want to be successful, we want to let our talents serve humanity, we want to find our true place in life, we want to progress. It is a natural desire of life to unfold through us. Therefore, your desire to be successful, to be happy, to be loved, and to live to your fullest potential is amazing. And you can achieve your goals if you educate yourself, discipline your thinking and feeling process, trust the Creator, and let yourself be the person you have always wanted to be. See yourself the way you want to be and start being it today. Think about yourself the way you want to be, and do it now. Love and appreciate yourself. Thank God and feel His presence, His love, His support, and His protection all the time. Feel the gratitude, calmness, satisfaction, and excitement of the answered prayer. Affirm positive ideas and Divine Truths, and you can reprogram your false beliefs, and remove the blocks that prevent you from achieving what you want. These practices will align you with your goals and give you the vibration that corresponds to what you want to achieve; they will help you to open up to the unlimited riches that you deserve.

You can read the following affirmations to focus on wealth, and to find your way to a more abundant life.

"Thank You God for Your unlimited
wealth that is in me! Thank You God that

Your infinite riches fill and overfill my life and me! Thank You for Your power in me. Thank You for Your might in me. Thank You for Your love and health that are in me, for Your happiness in me, for Your great power in me. Thank You for Your infinite Divine wealth and power that live in me, fill and overfill me, surround me and fill my whole life, everyone and everything that surround me. I swim in the eternal great Divine wealth. I enjoy these immense, generous, beautiful Divine gifts now and always! I am healthy, happy, loving, and loved. I am protected by God and His unlimited love! Thank You!

"*God loves and protects me. God surrounds me with love, safety, and protection. I can relax and trust that God will take care of everything. The whole world is kind, friendly, and helpful with God's help.*

"*Thank You God that right now my dreams, my fairytale, are coming true! Thank You for the huge, free, clean, kind, safe, and protected stream of wealth that bursts into my life right now! I swim in the unlimited Divine wealth right now and*

always! All my Divine dreams are coming
true right now! Thank You God! I love You!

"I believe that God fulfills my Divine and
most cherished dreams right now. Every day
I live it, I see and feel it! My most sincere
and Divine dreams and wishes are
manifesting and materializing right now!
Thank You! I love You!

"Thank You God that I am open and I
accept and receive Your Divine gifts now
and always. God's love, wealth and
protection fill all aspects of my life right now
and always! Thank You! I love You!

"Thank You God that my entire life is the
Divine happiness and love! Thank You for
enriching all aspects of my life with your
Divine, unlimited gifts! Thank You that I am
healthy, happy, wealthy, rich, loved, loving,
and calm! Thank You God for immense
wealth that You always send to my life!
Thank You God for Your Divine Love and
that Your love always fills my happy life!
Thank You that I am filled with health,
happiness, and love. Thank You that I am a
truly divinely happy and successful person!
Thank You!

"Thank You God for good health and happiness! Thank You God for my good and successful career and business! Thank You God for Your Divine wealth, which fills all aspects of my life! Thank You God for Your infinite Divine wealth that always fills my whole life! Thank You God for that I always trust You completely, in everything! I love You!

"Thank You God for Your constant protection and love. Thank You for always protecting my family and me! Thank You God for me always trusting You in everything, in all my deeds. Thank You God for Your great calmness that is always in me! I love You! Thank You!"

Feel free to add anything you want or anything you feel is lacking. Feel free to alter, edit, and correct these affirmations to tailor them for yourself. Feel free to expand these affirmations in any way your heart suggests to you.

"Thank You for showing me my way. Thank You for the great work, business or practice that came into my life so easy and fast! Thank You for Your great unlimited infinite wealth which always fills my life. Thank You for my good health, happiness,

reciprocal and happy love, for having a lot of free time, for my success, and for Your riches in me. Thank You for good friends, a great healthy and happy family, and love. Thank You for my successful career, for beauty, for my easy, free, calm, interesting, beautiful, wealthy, and healthy life. Thank You for interesting, successful, happy, good, real, and loyal friends! Thank You for real, true love. Thank You for the best spouse for me, and for my healthy, wealthy, and happy family. Thank You for Your Divine bliss and Your blessings! I love You! Thank You!

"Thank You God for Your infinite wisdom, for You leading and directing me. Thank You for Your blessings, for Your love and protection. Thank You for always showing me the answer. Thank You for the best and fastest outcome of this issue! Thank You for dealing with this problem and for taking care of everything. Thank You for the best results of this deal. Thank You!"

You can choose any of these affirmations, or maybe even all of them. You can expand on them, add to them, write your own affirmations, and repeat one or more of them for three to seven, or even more, times a day, for five to 10 minutes or more, for as long as it takes to change your negative beliefs about wealth or any aspect of your life into the ones that will actually help you in achieving your goals.

You can also use shorter affirmations to help yourself deal with negative thoughts throughout the day. If you cannot read your longer affirmation at a given moment, such as when you're in the car, in the store, at work, or at a meeting, but some disturbing negative thoughts pop into your head, you can still change them with another thought by focusing on what you want or inwardly repeating a short affirmation.

For example, a negative thought shows up, like: "I don't have enough money" or "I will never be able to afford it," or something else. You can change it with an opposite positive thought or affirmation such as: "With God's help I can do anything," "God's love fills my whole body, it fills me completely," or "God's love heals my body, my mind and my soul." These shorter phrases are easier to repeat when you are busy, and you can repeat them as many times as you need, even if you have to do it 100 or 2,000 times. Repeat it until your negative thought and feeling are changed. You can stop when you feel relaxed and calm, and when you know and feel that your prayer is answered.

We really give in to different convictions, and our subconscious mind can really be persuaded. We can easily be convinced by different ideas, news, and someone else's beliefs. The good thing here is that, if you know this, you can consciously choose what beliefs are good for you, are beneficial, and can lead to fulfillment of your goals, and also dispel those beliefs that are not good or beneficial for you. We should use our conscious mind to feed ourselves with truths that can serve us, benefit us, and help us in our achievements.

Even though we can consciously choose what information we need and what we don't need, sometimes it might be a good idea to make sure that you are not exposed to negative information which you can easily avoid. Pay attention to what you watch and listen to on TV, what programs you watch, what your friends talk about, what you read, and what you hear during the day. And if you can easily eliminate or avoid the negative stream of information, which you don't really need, it can be a good idea to do so.

Sometimes we cannot avoid some sources of negative information due to different factors. But don't get frustrated. It's okay. You are a conscious being and you always have a choice. You can choose what to believe and what to accept as a truth for you. And it does make more sense to always keep, absorb, listen to, and focus on things that actually serve you, help you in achieving your life plans, instead of focusing on something that will only disturb you, and block or prevent you from reaching your ultimate goals. By reading positive self-help literature and kind and friendly books and humorous stories, by watching positive and funny movies, self-improvement programs and DVD's, by talking about pleasant topics with your friends, you can help yourself stay in the positive mode.

Imagination is also very important in the creation process. All of us have this amazing gift of imagination. The question is, how do we use it? Again, you have a choice. You can consciously make sure that you are using this marvelous tool of imagination to your own advantage. When people worry about something, when they don't feel good, they tend to picture and visualize negative images in their mind, and sometimes they watch this negative film in their mind over and over again. The fear that something might or can happen makes people think and visualize different kinds of bad outcomes. First of all, most of our fears and things that we worry about, like losing a job, not being able to pay for something, not having enough, fear for people we love, and many other fears are not real. They will never come true. Nevertheless, we worry about those things. We do this because we want to avoid the bad outcome. We want to avoid and prevent bad outcomes and negative results; basically, we just want to protect ourselves.

What is important here is to understand that by worrying we cannot change anything anyway. The bad feelings, the feelings of fear, the feelings that we feel when we worry and when we are nervous, cannot protect us. When we imagine a hundred kinds of bad outcomes, we cannot change anything. We cannot change anything by worrying and imagining the bad result.

What we actually do is, as you already know, create what we think about during the day. We bring to our lives more of what we feel and think about. So, by being afraid and worrying, we don't do anything good. Our worries cannot protect us. Our negative imagination can only make us more afraid, more nervous and, as a result, more fragile.

Anyway, the right decisions and right actions come when we are calm. The clear, calm mind is a better adviser. When we are calm, there are more chances that we will make the right decisions than when we are nervous and troubled. When we are clear and calm, we can hear and feel the Divine Wisdom that is in us. Playing in your head and watching these negative pictures of unreal results don't prevent anything, they just make you focus on the wrong thing, on something opposite from what you actually want. Therefore, it is really important to discipline your imagination.

When we use our imagination, consciously choosing and focusing on what we want to think about, how we want to feel, and what we want to imagine, we turn on a powerful process of originative creation. We turn this power to work for our advantage. We use the Divine tools given to us in the right way and for the right purposes. And we can greatly benefit from disciplined thinking, disciplined feeling, and disciplined imagination.

Try to never picture anything bad or negative in your mind. If negative thoughts come up, try not to support them; change them with positive thoughts. If negative images start to rotate in your mind, change them to the opposite, to what you actually want — because in reality that's what you are actually trying to do.

We want this to happen, we want the desired outcomes to manifest in our lives; but instead of focusing on what we want and imagining it, and feeling good about it, we tend to focus on lack or on negative outcomes. We do this because we start to worry and we want to somehow prevent negative things and undesired outcomes from happening. But somehow, we find and use a very strange and illogical tool for that. Somehow, we decide to act in a manner opposite of what we want.

Instead, try to focus on what you do want. Focus on the desired outcome. Imagine what you want. Imagine the desired result and watch your feelings. Feelings are great indicators that show you where your focus is. If you feel good, you are focusing on what you want; if you feel bad, you are probably trying to imagine the car that you want, but you also have a thought in your head, somewhere deep within, that you don't have it, and might never get it. So, you actually focus on lack. Watch your feelings. The way you feel will reveal the true direction of your focus.

Think about your goals. Feel good and imagine the desired outcome. You can be creative. Imagine yourself the person you want to be, doing things you want to do, enjoying life, and feel good during this process of creative imagination. You can do this by relaxing and closing your eyes, or by dreaming about things you want to achieve. You can do this in the nature, for example near the sea or the ocean, or at home. It is not some special practice that you have to know how to do or learn. You use your imagination everyday anyway. Why not think about or imagine positive, pleasant things that can put you in a good mood and on the right track, and help you in achieving your goals?

Make sure that in your images you see yourself now, at the present moment. Don't think something like, "I will become successful next summer," "I'll be wealthy when I get a good job," "I'll feel happy when I get married," "I'll feel happy when I move to another place," or "I'll feel happy in the next 10 years."

When you are thinking about your dreams, when you practice creative imagination, see yourself the way you want to be, and see it now, like you already are the person you want to become: A successful businessman, a good wife, a famous actor, a happy and successful person. Don't leave anything for later. You can enjoy it now, in your thoughts and in your imagination.

And watch your feelings. Make sure you feel successful. Make sure you feel happy, feel good, and feel wealthy. Just say to yourself: "I am the person I want to be. I am happy, I am successful, I am…" and you can continue the list, with more things you want to be. And at the end you can say: "Thank You God!"

VI

THE RELATIONSHIP WITH YOURSELF

It is extremely important to have the right vision and feelings toward yourself. It is also crucial to have healthy self-esteem. You should already see yourself as the person you want to be, because you already are. You are the Divine being; part of the Divine is in you. You are created perfect. You are unique; there is no one else like you in this entire world. The Life Principle expresses itself through you. You are the beloved child of God. You should know it, you should feel it. The way you think about yourself, the thoughts you have about yourself, your image about yourself, the words you say about yourself, the way you feel about yourself, your impression about yourself are all important, because, remember, what you think about you bring into your life. Therefore, your thoughts and feelings toward yourself should only be positive, should be filled with love and self respect; you should respect yourself as a Divine being. You are God's child, so respect and love yourself as you are God's perfect creation.

Feel that you deserve all the best in life. How can you get something good if you don't think you deserve it, if you would not even give it to yourself? Feel that you deserve love, that you deserve wealth, health, beauty. You

47

deserve to be happy, wealthy. You deserve the best spouse for you. You deserve all the riches that life can offer. You deserve respect, a good career, good friends, good health, self-improvement, love. You really deserve all the best in life. You should feel it, you should know it. Know your worth. Know that you are amazing, because you really and truly are! How could God create something or someone who is not perfect? You are His perfect and beloved child! Rejoice, be happy, enjoy every minute of your life, for every second of it is sacred.

You are amazing; there is no one else like you in the entire world. God created you perfect. He gave you unique talents, gifts. There is no one else like you. You are God's beloved child. There is part of the Divine in you; so love yourself, love this part of the Divine that is in you. You are the Divine being. Love yourself, respect yourself the way you are. How can you expect someone else to love and respect you if you don't feel these feelings toward yourself? You deserve love. God loves you; and He takes care of you all the time. Feel the love and respect towards this beautiful, amazing and perfect child of God: Yourself. Love yourself. Feel the feelings of love and gratitude toward yourself. Love the way you look, the things you do, the way you act, the way you think. And if there is something that you are not proud about, something that you are not happy about from the past, that you have said or done, forgive yourself. All of these things are gone; they are in the past. What really matters is the present, this moment, right now. See yourself the way you want to be.

See yourself in the new vision, see yourself the way you you've always wanted to be, see and feel it now.

Thank God for creating you, thank Him for your life, for this day, for this second. Ask God for forgiveness, and forgive yourself. God always forgives you. When you come to Him, He will always embrace you with His love and understanding. Remember: God always forgives you. He loves you. So, forgive yourself and feel this Divine Love that always surrounds you. Respect this love and love yourself. Be thankful for this unconditional love that God gives you, and love yourself unconditionally. Love the part of the Divine in you. Forgive yourself. Let go of all the guilt and fear, let go of the past. The past is gone; the only thing that matters is this moment, how you live it, how you feel, what you think, how you see yourself, what you think about the world, what you believe in. Forgive yourself, love yourself, think about yourself, and see yourself as the person you want to be. Do it now.

Focus your thoughts and feelings on positive things — on love, gratitude, wellbeing, good health, wealth, happiness. You already know that what you think about you bring into your life, you attract it. You have the choice. So, attract only the best in life; be happy and love yourself, love this life. Love everyone around you, and fill yourself with these immense riches that the Universe has for you. Open yourself to love, and love will flood your life, love will fill you, your heart, your soul, your mind, everything around you. God's love will heal you; it will heal all aspects of your life, because you are the beloved child of

God. And He is always with you. God loves you, helps you, protects you, and leads you to whatever is perfect and right for you.

When you truly love yourself, when you feel respect towards yourself, when you feel that you deserve all the best in life, then you possess real and true self-esteem. And I am not talking about ego, or feelings of supremacy. People have these "unhealthy" feelings of superiority when they lack the most important thing that gives them the feeling of completeness — the feeling of oneness with the Infinite Intelligence that is within us.

When we lose — or maybe it is better to say when we don't realize this connection (because we cannot really lose it; it is always there, whether we think about it or not) — we don't feel complete, we don't feel satisfied. And to compensate for that, people start to look for some artificial means, and they try to substitute this need, this thirst for Love (which is our Divine nature), with something else, something artificial. Our Divine nature always calls us to our origin, to the Source, to what is real, to who we truly are. People try to find the missing part that they feel they really need, but some people try to find it in the wrong places. They try to find comfort in alcohol and other unhealthy pleasures. Others feel the need for power, for a good position in society, to please their ego. They feel this emptiness inside, and they try to replace it with something that their ego feels might help them.

But usually, these "unhealthy" pleasures, and temporary satisfaction of the ego, do not fill the real gap, do not really give or do what these people are looking for. These people cannot find what their souls long for and what they feel the lack of, because they are looking for the wrong thing and in the wrong place. They try to find this inner sense of fulfillment, happiness, love, and sense of wholeness outside of themselves. They are afraid to look inside. Because to do so, you need to stay one-on-one with yourself and listen to this inner child inside of you, to the cry of your soul, to the things inside that bother you, to this dissatisfaction that's gathered there through the years. And people are afraid of looking into the eyes of their souls, of staying one-on-one with their pain.

But just shutting it down, shutting down this pain, does not eliminate it. It just makes it worse. You just sprinkle it with dust and hide it deep inside, underneath the nicely polished surface. But you cannot ignore yourself, you cannot ignore the call of your soul. The only thing that can heal is love, the Divine Love. And nothing artificial can ever substitute, even closely, for what you really long for.

And what we all are really looking for is this Divine Love, this source of the infinite, unlimited, unconditional love that actually is our nature. The Divine Love that God gives us. The protection, quite calmness and satisfaction, which only this connection can give - when we love God, when we love ourselves, when we love the Divine in us, when we feel the Everlasting Infinite Almighty Presence all around us and inside of us. This connection to the Divine is what we are truly looking for. This gives the real sense of fulfillment. We feel whole and complete, when we know, feel, maintain, and live in this connection, when we are connected to the Source and when we completely trust the Divine, and when we are completely open to the love, care, protection and riches of the Only Power that is – the Infinite Presence, which is in us and which is in everything that is. God's love and protection is always with you, remember about it.

This conscious love towards yourself, this respect towards the part of the Divine that is in you, this is a real basis for a real and true self-esteem. This love towards yourself and self-esteem do not need any support of any outside factors, they don't need anybody's approval, they don't depend on anything outside of you. The only support you need is your support, your belief in yourself, your love towards yourself, feeling of your own worthiness, and God's support. God always loves you. He always supports you. You are His beloved child. When you have this kind of love towards yourself, this kind of self-respect and self-esteem, it is impossible to lose it, because it does not depend on any circumstances, it does not depend on any situation, on anything outside of you. You don't need to prove anything, to reach anything, in order to love and respect yourself. You don't even have to look for this self-esteem, because it is always there, it is always inside of you. It always exists, and it is real, it is true. Feel the feelings of love, and respect towards yourself. Feel and believe that you are worth all the best in life, that you deserve to love and to be loved, that you deserve all the gifts and riches that the Universe has for you. Always remember that God loves you, He always protects you, supports you, leads and directs you. He is always by your side. Be happy, be calm and feel the feelings of love and gratitude towards yourself and everything that is. Be thankful, love the Creator, love yourself, love everything that exists and be happy.

It is very important to know and remember that God loves you. God wants you to live a better life and have everything you need. God wants you to be happy; He takes care of you, He protects you. He guides you throughout your entire life. Some people believe that poverty and suffering is the will of God for them. God loves us, unconditionally, He forgives us. The part of the Divine is in us. He always supports us. He gave us the talents, He gave us this life for us to live and enjoy it. God wants us to prosper, to be healthy, to be wealthy, to be loved, to be happy. How can the loving Father want something else for His beloved child, for His perfect creation? *"Is there anyone among you who, if your child asks for a fish, will give a snake instead of a fish? Or if the child asks for an egg, will give a scorpion?"* (Luke 11:11-12)

God loves us unconditionally, and there is no greater love in the Universe than His. You don't have to worry about anything. The Life Principle expresses itself through you. It always goes forward, to the higher level of being. It pushes you to achieve even greater heights, to reach even taller mountains of your success and self-improvement, to express yourself to the fullest of your potentials, to express the talents that are given to you, to serve the humanity to the best of your ability, to live the best life possible, to feel the joy and the bliss of the Universe, to flourish, and come closer to the Divine nature of you and everything that is. It always leads you forward, higher, to where you belong, to the Source of everything, to God. The God's will for you is to be happy, healthy, wealthy, successful, loved and to experience all the best in life.

God loves you. He always supports you, He takes care of you, He is always by your side. He always surrounds you with His unlimited, unconditional love, the kind of love, which is beyond any imagination possible. You should always remember this. You should always know that the love of God and His support are with you. If your deeds are good deeds, if your desires are the desires that lead to self-improvement, personal growth, wellness, and wellbeing of yourself and others, the whole Universe supports you. You should believe and know that you deserve all the best in life, that you are worth it, and that the God's will for you is to prosper, be happy, healthy, blissful, wealthy and joyous. Open yourself to the Divine Truths. Let go of your worries. Trust the Divine. Follow your heart and allow yourself to be happy and to receive all the riches the life has for you.

VII

THE POWER WITHIN YOURSELF

You should know and feel the power within yourself. You have the power, the strength to change the circumstances. You should know and believe that you have the power to achieve and mount anything you want in life. The part of the Divine is in you. You should know and feel the power of the Divine within. You should know and feel that you are capable of achieving your goals, that you can and will become the person you want to be because you already are that person. There is nothing impossible for God, and He is always with you. He is always by your side, His support is with you. Everything already exists in our infinite Universe. All we need to do is to allow ourselves experience the beauty and riches of life, to let these Divine gifts in your existence, to open ourselves to the unlimited, unconditional love and all the blessings that it brings with it, to open the door and let the triumph and success into our habitat.

You should always know that God is on your side. When you desire happiness, personal growth, prosperity, and wellbeing for yourself and everyone else, when your dreams are good in their nature and are focused on bringing even more good and serving humanity, then the entire

Universe is on your side. You should know and believe that God is helping you and will always help you. His unlimited, Almighty Power is with you, and it is within you. *"If God is for us, who is against us?"* (Romans 8:31) Know and believe in the Power of God, in his love and support. Know and believe in the Divine Power within you, and live to your fullest potential.

The biggest mistake that we usually make is that we look at our circumstances, at the situation around us, and we give the power to external factors, to the people, situations, and things that surround us. Therefore, we blame everyone and everything for our misfortunes and failures. Often, people say that they cannot find a good job, because they don't have the right connections, or because they don't have enough knowledge or education, that they are not successful because their parents did not give them enough freedom, enough of this or enough of that, that they are unhappy because their spouse would not let them become the person they want to be, or to do the things they like doing.

The biggest mistake is to give the power to someone or something else. It is your power. The Divine Power is within you, it is inside of you, and until you understand you have it, until the moment you feel it, the outer world will dictate the rules and you will suffer, feeling helpless. As soon as you shift your mental attitude and understand that the power to build your life, to construct whatever you want in your life is in God's hands, it is in His power, and it is in the Divine Power that is inside of you, you will be able to change your circumstances. They will no longer rule your life. You will become the creator, supported by the Almighty Power of the Divine.

God created you, He enriched you with His talents, with unique abilities that only you possess. He loves and supports you. He wants you to succeed, flourish and reach the top. He wants you to grow and self-improve. There is the part of the Divine in you. The power of the Devine is in you, and you enable and lead this power with your thoughts and feelings. And you choose whether to use it or not and how to use it. It is a gift to you from the Creator. He gave you the power to create your destiny and He gave you the choice. What you need to understand is that God loves you, protects you, supports you, and leads you to the perfect outcome, to whatever is perfect and right for you.

Many people never think about this and they allow the mass mind to control them. They never think about what they create with their thoughts and feelings. They never focus their feelings and thoughts on positive outcomes. They think and feel whatever their brain is fed by media, information they read about or hear on the streets and opinions of others. They allow the thoughts of masses and opinions of others fill their minds, and create the results they are not happy with. If the person does not consciously choose his thoughts and feelings, and if he gets lucky, some positive information can govern him and he will attract some good experiences, without even knowing how that have happened, but very often, the unfiltered information is negative. And if the person takes it and accepts it as his own belief, and lives with it, thinks about it, and feels it, he or she attracts some negative circumstances to his or her life. The person attracts what he thinks about; he attracts circumstances that correspond to the nature of his thoughts and feelings. This is all very natural, we all do it. This is why some people get lucky and some people don't, some people get rich and some people don't, some people are happy and some people are not.

There are many people who, maybe, are happy and wealthy, even without consciously learning about these laws of the Universe, but if you ask them what they actually do, they would probably say that they dream about their goals, they are always or most of the time in a happy and positive mood, before they go to bed they thank for everything they have and they imagine every tomorrow even better than yesterday. They expect good things to happen. They are applying these laws without even knowing they do it. They do it naturally, maybe because the circumstances around them help them in it. Or maybe because they attracted a few good things and really believed in their ability to achieve their goals, make money, make friends, and be successful. Some people just know that they are successful, that they are attractive, that they are wealthy, that they are the best. Maybe, their parents or grandparents taught them that, and they really have believed in it from their childhood.

The interesting idea is that, it is more beneficial to actually, consciously know about the laws that govern the

Universe and our lives, and apply them consciously, rather than accidentally. Have you heard stories, or maybe you know some people, who started from scratch and they became very successful, achieved everything they wanted — and then something happened and they lost everything? Some of them were able to achieve the same or even greater heights after their failure, but some of them could not reach the same standards of living again.

This, most likely happened, because at the beginning, when they just started their road to success, they were young, they believed in their power, strength, in their ability to build a successful life for themselves and their family, therefore, they focused on success. They worked hard and they achieved it. And then something happened. They already had everything they wanted and they shifted their focus to the opposite. They grew afraid that they could lose it. They did not focus their attention on the happy future and success anymore. All they wanted was to preserve and keep everything they had, their comfortable luxurious lifestyle. And the fear of losing everything they worked for so hard and so long came to dominate their thoughts and feelings. This shift in their attitude could happen because of many reasons. Maybe as they grew older they became afraid that they were not so productive anymore. Or maybe they moved to a different country and grew afraid that they would not be able to achieve the same heights in the new country. Or maybe there was no "real" reason at all, and they just made it up. (Sometimes people start to worry without any obvious or real reason.). Who knows? That's not the point. The point, though, is that the negative shift occurred.

So, the shift from positive, successful thinking and feeling process to the thoughts and feelings of lack, preservation and fear of losing, attracted what they were afraid of, and they, eventually, lost everything. They actually attracted lack, because they were focused on lack. And most likely this happened, because they never applied the laws of attraction consciously. They did not know about these laws, or maybe they knew, but ignored them and they just followed whatever was suggested to them from the outside. They did not consciously apply the laws. They did not consciously choose the thoughts and feelings, and their experiences followed and corresponded to the nature of their thoughts, which were not consciously chosen, which were accidental.

When the person knows the laws that govern his or her life and when he or she consciously applies these laws of the Universe, when the person consciously chooses what to think about and how to feel, how to focus, discipline and lead his or her thinking process, the person can create, with God's help, the results, happiness, success, bliss and wealth beyond anything he or she can imagine.

Never give (in your mind) any power to the outside factors, people or circumstances. You should always know and remember that the power is within you. There is only one power in this Universe, the Power of God. God is the only power that exists. The part of the Divine is in you, and the power of the Devine is in you too. The Creator loves, supports and leads you, and you activate the Divine Power within you, by focusing your thought and feeling process on things you want to attract to your life, by trusting God and letting go of negativity and attachment to the result, and by anticipating the best results possible, and by feeling thankful and calm, because you know that your prayer is already answered. So, there is only one power in this Universe, and it is the power of the Almighty, and the Divine Power within yourself. How can you then say that your neighbor's hate can bring you bad luck, that someone's curse can make you suffer, that the envy and the bad eye of some other person can influence how you feel, how you live, or what you have?

Never give the power to the outer things, events, circumstances, and to others. When you dream about wellness and wellbeing for yourself and others, when your desires are about good and positive things, when they are filled with love and care, when you wish yourself and others all the best, the power of the Almighty supports you, God supports and leads you. There is only one power in this world. It is the power of the Creator and His Divine Power in you. You are free, you are safe. The Almighty Power of God is with you, the power of the Divine is in you. You were born to succeed, you were born to triumph, you were born to thrive, you were born to win. The life expresses itself through you and it is in its nature to achieve its highest potential, to reach the highest goals and to swim in the ocean of success and wealth. You have no other choice but to win; for the Power of the Almighty is with you. The Divine Power is within you. Relax, trust God and discipline your thinking and feeling process. Never give the power in your head to anything or anybody else. This was the false belief; change it, and remember that there is only one power in this Universe: The Almighty Power of God — and that power is with you, and it is inside of you.

Do not react negatively on anything from the outside. Remain calm and focused on your ideas, your positive beliefs, your goals. Don't worry about your neighbors, friends, relatives, coworkers. Don't worry about what they say, think or do. Don't let anybody and anything make you lose your balance, your focus, your calmness. Don't allow the outer circumstances to decrease your faith, don't allow them to lead you into the opposite direction from where you are going. If you allow your five senses to rule you, if you allow the outer circumstances, events and people rule your thinking and feeling process, you will allow the fear to rule you. Fear is the opposite of love. Love creates, blesses, inspires and heals. Fear confuses and messes things up. At first it creates frustration, instability, and uncertainty in your thoughts and feelings, and later in your reality.

No matter how the life looks like today, and what your five senses tell you, your present reality is only the outcome of your past thoughts, feelings, and reactions. What is important is this moment right now. And right now you should remember that you decided to achieve your goals, to become the person you want to be, to be happy and wealthy. You have made this decision, and you should discipline your thinking and feeling process and work towards manifesting and materializing your goals, and dreams. Don't allow anyone or anything to disturb this process, your mission. Stay focused no matter what. And remember, that there is only one power. And this power is on your side, it is with you, it is within you. And there is nothing stronger than this power. It is the Almighty Power of God.

The Power of God governs your life. You are surrounded by His love, protection and care, and there is a Divine kingdom of love, beauty and perfection within you. Cherish it, be thankful for it, love it and remain loyal to your position in life and you will be greatly rewarded, because you will reap the harvest of your own thoughts, beliefs and ideas. You will be inspired to the right actions. The Almighty Power will open any door for you and give you any riches, if you allow yourself to accept these riches and open yourself to it, and if you trust, and allow this Power to bring the happiness, wealth, health, joy, love, bliss, success and triumph, which are far beyond any imagination possible. And remember, you are not along. The Creator is always by your side. What other support can you possibly need, and what can be impossible for His Almighty Power? Trust His lead and walk the road of happiness, wealth, success and love, protected by the gentle and loving arm of the Infinite Presence.

VIII

GOOD THINGS JUST HAPPEN IF YOU LET THEM

When you stay calm and focused on your goal, when you discipline your thinking and feeling process, when you let go of all worries and focus only on positive thoughts and feelings, when you practice affirmations, work on yourself and stay aligned with these positive vibrations, with time, positive things will just happen. Usually, these positive results pop up when you don't expect them, when you don't try hard. Sometimes, they are completely surprising. They can be completely different from what you imagine. Even though, you might be surprised by the results, it will always be in a good way (it will always be a pleasant surprise) and the feeling you will get from these results will be as good as you desired or even better. Sometimes, you don't even have to do anything to get the result you want, it will just happen. It will come from the most unexpected source and might have the most unexpected form, but you will always be contented and happy with it.

At times, while the end result, your big desire, is still in the process of creation, some other amazing events or things can happen, that will pleasantly surprise you, they can happen in different areas of your life, even if you did not really think about them. Sometimes, the plan turns out to be different than you expected, sometimes, completely different, but you will find that the way it turns out, is much better than you could even imagine. Universe might line up different surprising pleasant events that will actually lead you to that big outcome. The main idea here is that when you are ready, when you align your vibrations with the desired outcome, and when your mind, your feelings and your inner self are ready, the answer just comes. The result will show up, it will just happen. Very often, you don't even have to do anything for that, it is that easy. At times, you will get a quick and complete result; and sometimes it will manifest itself slowly, bringing other positive changes on the way in. Sometimes it can happen very fast, and sometimes it might take time. Don't worry about it. Know and believe, feel that your prayer is answered and it will just happen.

You can always help this process of positive thought transformation with some other physical actions. It is always good to remember about the balance in life. We should always think about balance in all aspects of our life and about improving all parts of us. Therefore, while we work and discipline our mind, thoughts and feelings, we should also remember about our body. It is always nice to stay physically active and fit. In order to feel better, look better, to be more energized and productive we have to be physically active. For that, we can go for a walk, sit outside, and spend time in the nature. So, while we work on the positive transformation of our thoughts and feelings, it will also be very helpful to discipline the body too. Check with your doctor what exercises are good for your health and sign up for some aerobics or yoga classes, gymnastics, ballet, belly dancing, swimming, tennis. See what better works for you, if these sports are not the right choice, you can just simply go for a walk, spend time outside, go to the park, forest or beach and enjoy the nature. Surprisingly, but physical exercises also help to increase self-esteem, to improve self-confidence and to feel better about yourself. Physical exercises help with our thinking process, they help to release negative thoughts and feelings, and they also train our body, muscles and help to stay fit. Any kind of discipline, when it is in the right amount, is pretty beneficial too. Body discipline will also help you discipline your thoughts.

Think about how organized are your life, your schedule, and your time management. Are you organized? Are your life and work organized? Is your working place organized? How do you manage your time? The right thinking process will help to organize your physical things and activities. And vice versa when your life is organized, it will also help to organize your thinking process. Everything in this life is interconnected. It does not mean that you have to try to control and organize everything. Keep it easy, simple, enjoy it, and apply just the right amount of self-discipline and organization. Don't be too hard on yourself, but don't ignore this process either. Deep inside, if you listen to your deeper mind, to your inner voice, we are all guided by the Divine wise guidance, so we all can feel what we should do, how and to what extend we should do one or another thing, because all of us are unique and different. Therefore, no one knows what is good and right for you, better than the Divine in you. You are guided and led by God, and He always knows what is perfect and right for you.

Don't worry. Don't feel overwhelmed, that there are too many things that need to be changed and so many aspects in life that need some improvement or some work to be done. Don't worry about that. We are here to improve ourselves, to always move forward, to the top, to God. We are here to express our best qualities and live our life to our fullest potential. It is an infinite and never ending process. You made a decision and began this process of positive transformation, enjoy every step of it. The things you have in your life now, are the results of your past thinking and feeling process, but the moment you stop following the habitual negative thought pattern, and you fill yourself with positive thoughts, feelings, beliefs and Divine Truth, you start a new road, road to success, and you create new experiences of success, wealth, happiness, triumph and bliss. Be thankful and amazed of every second of your existence. Bless every experience and everything you have in your life. All of this is an amazing gift, the gift of life. Enjoy it to the fullest, live it to the best and be this amazing person you truly are. Stop hiding under the masks of fear, lack and limitations. You are the Divine being. The part of the Divine is in you. The Life Principle expresses itself through you. You are an amazing, unique, Divine being. The power of the Almighty is always by your side. You are always surrounded by unlimited and unconditional love of God. His constant support and protection are always with you.

We all know that our life is not constant it is an ever-changing process. Therefore, the fluctuation is normal, fluctuation of feelings, and fluctuation of the results. Everyone has their ups and downs, so, it is important to stay focused on your goals, on positive thoughts and feelings, no matter what. It is important to stay determined, to stay loyal to your decision, to your dreams and goals, even when it feels that nothing is happening, that changes are not occurring, when it feels that things go wrong, when it feels that this does not work, or when something happens, which is not quite the thing you wanted to happen.

During our positive transformation process there might be some bumps on the road, they don't have to be, but there might be. Some of them can be bigger and some can be smaller, so be prepared. Don't allow anything to disturb you and to distract you from your focus, from your goal, from your goal to be wealthy, to be happy, to be successful.

Sometimes, people read positive books, work on their self-improvement, work on making their thinking and feeling process more positive, practice affirmations and meditation, attend lectures. They do everything they can (at least they think so), but results are not manifesting. During the moments when you feel that you are trying hard and it does not work, don't allow the negative thoughts to enter, don't allow them to ruin your prior work. Stay calm, stay determined, and know that the answer is coming. Everything already exists in this Universe and if you do not see it yet, it does not necessary mean it's not there. Like the stars, we don't see them during the day, but they are there, up in the sky. You just have to wait until the night comes, to see them with your own eyes.

In the moment when you feel that results are not coming and that everything remains the same, shift your focus, choose again, choose what you want, choose love, confidence, trust and faith. Know that your prayer is already answered. It is answered before you even asked, because God knows what you need even better than you do. He created you, He knows what is perfect and right for you. All you have to do is to focus consciously on the positive thoughts, on the thoughts of wealth, on feeling good, on feeling wealthy. Know and feel that you already are the person you always wanted to be. And you have to continue this process until it becomes a conviction, until you believe in it, until it sinks into your subconscious.

Know that you can do it. Know that you have the power and ability in you to do it. God gave you this gift, use it wisely. Choose what you want — choose happiness, wealth, abundance, health, joy, prosperity, bliss, success. You can choose anything your soul longs for. Focus on it, and trust the love of Creator. His Almighty Power, support and protection are always with you, and there is nothing more stable, stronger, wiser and more loving than this Almighty Presence that is always by your side.

The feeling of ease is also very important part of the manifestation process. Let go of your desire, let go of the desired outcome. It is hard to describe the right feeling with the words, it's the same as describing how the peach tastes to someone who has not even seen it. That's why, while many authors write about it, it is not that easy for people to understand and grasp it on the level of feeling. But what's important, is the feeling of ease. Don't try too hard, do not be desperate. Let go of any feeling of need. Very calm and light thoughts and feelings, which indicate that you want this particular thing is enough, is great.

There should not be any worry or thinking about how to get it, when you will get it, how it will come into your life. And you don't even have to think about your goal all day, or for three hours, you can do that, if you want (at times it can be a pretty good practice too), but you don't have to. Sometimes, it can be enough to look at something, have a slight thought that indicates that you want it, and feel the calm and easy feeling of peace, and slight feeling that you "will and already have it." 'I already have it' idea gives you calmness and peace of possession. This idea will help you to relax and understand that you are not lying to yourself, about the desired outcome. It will help you to have this true feeling that you already have what you want.

This is, already, too much of explanation. You don't even have to know how it works and how it feels, and this process might also vary from time to time. All you have to remember is to let go of any need, let go of the end result, let go of feelings of fear or worrying about not getting what you want, or worrying about how to get it, or when. Just ease, peace, calmness, certainty, slight anticipation, thankfulness, and stable emotion, thought and feeling of certainty and calmness, because you know that your prayer is already answered, because you know that the result or the thing that you want is already yours. And you know this, not because you are really trying to imagine it to be yours, but because you just know it deep inside. You know, that it is for you and it is yours. And it will just happen.

In some cases, you have to act, you have to do something in order to achieve the desired outcome, and don't worry you will be guided. But sometimes you don't even have to do anything, just receive your dream in reality. At times, when you have a very strong desire for something and you've been waiting for a long time to get it, you have to let go of the desired outcome, to the extent that you don't even care anymore. You still might have the slight focus on it in your head, but you don't care how it will be done, what the result will be, how and when it will come about. You don't even care. This feeling of ease and letting go, opens you up, cleans all the blocks, and the Divine energy flows freely. You become an open channel that is ready to receive all the riches that the generous and bountiful Universe has for you.

IX

THE "RULE" OF LOVE

There is another thing that you need to know. There is an important rule to this process of manifestation of happiness, balanced life and your dreams. We need to treat others the way we would treat ourselves, we have to wish to others what we would wish ourselves, be filled with love and goodwill towards ourselves and others. This is an important rule that we cannot and should not forget about. We have to eliminate jealousy, hate, envy and negative emotions towards other people. If you want to attract wealth, you have to feel good about any display of wealth around you and in the world. If you see expensive things that others possess, beautiful cars in the city, amazing luxurious houses, when you look at them, you have to have positive emotions. How do you usually feel when you hear about wealthy people, when you hear about their achievements, about their possessions? If you feel bad or uncomfortable, if you have any, even little, slight feelings of envy, that means, that in your mind you are focused on lack. You start to feel bad, because you know you don't have it, while the other person has. But, remember, you are the beloved child of God. There is immense wealth all around you. Our Universe is unlimited, it is full of amazing beautiful riches, it is bountiful. Can you count how many leafs are on the trees, how many stars are there at night, how many flowers are in the fields, how many clouds are up in the sky, how many drops of water are in the ocean? God always provides us with an unlimited wealth. It is here, it is everywhere, so allow yourself to have it. All we need to do is to open up to these unlimited riches that are all around us.

Therefore, feel good for others. Be happy to see the wealth of the world. Welcome it with a smile and happiness, be a good host. Welcome wealth and abundance of the world with hospitality, with open arms and happy feelings. Be happy to see, that one more person did allow himself or herself to drink from this never ending source of unlimited abundance and love. Be happy that someone else could do it. It means and shows you that it is possible, that you can do it, too, because there is a part of the Divine in each and every one of us. The love of God is with us, His help and support are with us. Just allow yourself to be happy, wealthy and prosperous. Eliminate your own limitation in your own mind and open yourself to the unlimited riches of the Universe, and receive them with trust, love and gratitude.

Be happy for your friends and relatives who achieve their goals, buy new things, reach the heights. Be happy to see the other person happy, to see your friend or relative become wealthy and succeed in life. Be genuinely happy when your colleague gets a raise, or a better position, or buys a new car, or a house, or a ring, a watch, jewelry or clothes. Be happy when someone is healthy, happy, joyous, when someone looks good, handsome or beautiful. Be happy to see the dreams of others come true.

First of all, these good things are an amazing indicator that wealth is all around you, because we create and attract all circumstances in our life. You attracted this person to your life, and you attracted that you see this person succeed. This already means that you surrounded yourself with wealthy, happy and successful people, even if they are not your friends, and even if you don't have good relationship with them. It does not matter. You can see wealth and happiness all around you. First, wealth shows up by your side and then in your living room. So, you have to embrace this experience and be happy to see the happiness and success of others.

And secondly, you already know, that what you think about and how you feel, you attract. And when you feel good about others, about their wealth, success and possessions and you wish them even greater health, happiness, wealth and success, you focus on it, you focus on these positive things. You feel good, and that's what you create for yourself, that's what you attract into your own existence, into your life. You are becoming one more happy, successful and wealthy person on this planet. And finally, when you feel good, when you are in the state of love, gratitude, calmness and happiness, when you don't allow hate, jealousy and envy to poison your life, you eliminate the negativity. And love, the Divine Love, which is in you, which goes through you, creates miracles in all aspects of life.

Be happy for anyone, even if you think that you don't like the person, or the person does not like you, even if you think, this person does not deserve the riches and happiness he or she has, even if you hate that person or the person hates you, be happy for that person.

This gives rise to another issue: We should eliminate the feelings of hate, or negative feelings and thoughts towards anybody. No matter what has happened, if there is a reason or if there is no reason for that feeling, eliminate it, dissolve it completely. We are all beloved children of our Father. There is a part of the Divine in each and every one of us. We are Divine parts of the Whole. We need to see the Divine in every person and love everything that exists. Of course, we are human beings and we can have different reactions and attitude on the outside, from time to time, but deep inside we should feel this immense unlimited love towards ourselves and others. We should live in this Divine Love, feel it, think it, live it and be it.

When you make plans, wishes, when you dream, these dreams, your goals should come out of love, the Divine Love towards yourself, the world and others. God is love, infinite, unconditional, unlimited, boundless love. Align yourself with this genuine, deep and immense love of the Universe and it will heal all your worries, troubles, lack and limitations, your pain, and your negative feelings. The Divine Love will heal your mind and your soul, and it will allow you to see the world in the new light, and to live your dreams, inspired by the Infinite Intelligence, here and now. Each of your goals and plans should be filled with love and you should always be guided by and follow this rule: 'Do and whish for others what you will do and whish for yourself,' and you will be aligned with the Creating Power of the Universe and your happiness and goodwill towards others will multiply infinitely in your life. Open yourself to unlimited beauty, love, wealth, success, bliss, joy and triumph of the Universe, and live the life beyond any imagination possible. God can do anything, everything is possible for Him. He knows you the best, He created you. He loves you. Everything you will ever need is already here, it already exists, it is all for you. Open yourself to the unlimited love and care, to the infinite wellbeing, to the riches, wealth and abundance, to the happiness and success, and the Universe will enjoy and smile with you, being happy for the amazing things you can create, experience and enjoy, inspired by the Almighty wisdom, as you are filled by the unlimited, infinite and boundless love of the Creator.

Allow yourself to have everything you want. If you let yourself have it, the Universe will bring it you. It does not matter for the Universe to give you 1 cent or $1,000,000. The only limitations we have are ours, they are in our head. We know that we cannot have it, we don't mentally allow ourselves to have it, we think it is not possible. We question everything, our ability, the process, how it will happen or when. We don't think and feel we deserve it, we say that it is not for us, or "I don't have it", or "I can't have it." We make these mental blocks for ourselves in our heads. We mentally put limitation to the unlimited nature of life. All you have to do is to mentally allow yourself to be happy, to accept all the beauty, love, and riches the Universe has for us.

Let go of the result. Let go of the feeling of need and desperation. Fill yourself with ease, the Divine freedom, unconditional love, unlimited wealth, unlimited potential, happiness, bliss and joy, and the Universe will bring it for you. Be ready to receive it, be ready inside, and when your mind is ready, when you are ready, it will just happen surprisingly amazing, easy and with love. Allow yourself, let yourself in your mind to have what you want, remove the limitations in your mind and enjoy the bountiful gifts that are here for you. Just open the door of your mind, just let these gifts, these riches of the Universe into your life, just receive them with trust, love, ease and gratitude. Be happy, be wealthy, be successful. You deserve it. Allow yourself, let yourself have what you want, let yourself be happy, healthy, wealthy, prosperous, successful, beautiful, loved and joyous, and you will be surprised and amazed of what the Love can do, and how it can give. Let the unlimited potential of the Infinite Presence express itself through you and open you to the experiences beyond any imagination possible. Love can do it, you can do it and you are doing it right now. Allow yourself and let yourself be happy, wealthy, successful and blissful. Open up, be ready in your mind and receive with trust, love, calmness and gratitude.

There is another important point that we need to realize and think about. Of course, we should educate ourselves, do the research, learn new ideas from the people who know more than we do, in order to continue our self-improvement, but the most important thing here is that we need to find our own path, our own way. There is wisdom of the Divine in us. We need to learn to listen to it, recognize it and respect it. There is the power of the Almighty within us. We need to learn to apply and consciously use it to our advantages. There is a boundless, perpetual and unconditional love of the Infinite Presence within us and we need to feel it. There is a constant, ever-present guidance, care, love and support of the loving Creator by our side. We need to realize it, feel it and know about it. This will give you the feelings of trust, calmness, peace, and joy, because you will know and feel that you are always surrounded by the love, care, support, and help of the Almighty. You will feel that your prayer is already answered, even before you ask.

We are here to realize who we are, to realize and find the connection to the Divine within us, to feel and realize the connection to the Creator, His love and guidance. We are here to look within, to realize and feel the wisdom of Infinite within us, to be at peace with ourselves, to realize our true nature, beyond our five senses and what we can see, feel and experience here on this planet. We are here to live, to be happy, joyous, wealthy, to open our fullest potential and to reach the top of our own success. We are always asked and led to look inside, to the roots.

We are always led to the Source and to establishing, feeling and realizing our connection with the Source, the Infinite Presence.

We need to understand who we really are. We need to realize our true nature. We need to realize that we are the Divine beings and that there is a part of the Divine in us. No matter what you do or what you read, or what you are suggested to practice, ask yourself – "How do I feel about it?" Listen to your feelings, your inner self knows better than anybody else what is better for you. Trust the Infinite Presence and you will be guided towards what is perfect and right for you. Determine your own process of self-improvement, of spiritual growth and follow the higher lead, the Infinite wisdom within you. Open to this Infinite Presence within you, to its wisdom and realize that you are more than your body, more than your mind, more than anything your five senses can suggest. Realize your true Divine nature. Self-improve, learn more, explore, do the research, grow spiritually and always remember to determine and form your own beliefs and opinions, based on the higher guidance and the Infinite wisdom within you. You are complete, whole individual, who has everything he or she can ever need within yourself, when you realize and feel your connection to the Source, when you feel God's unconditional, unlimited love, His constant protection, support and care.

X

GO DEEPER THAN THE SURFACE

Here is another important thing, which we often don't even think about. When we want to create something, to attract the desired results, of course, it is great if we change our beliefs and thoughts about that particular aspect that we are trying to work on, but it is also important to know that we need to go deeper than that. For example, if we want to create wealth, prosperity and abundance in our life, it is great when we change our negative beliefs about wealth, when we focus our positive thoughts on our goal, but it is also important to know that we need to go deeper than just thoughts, beliefs and feelings about wealth. Everything in our life is interconnected. It is difficult to make perfect one aspect of life while another aspect is a total mess. Therefore, it is very helpful to also look at other mental blocks that you might have. It is important to look at and work on our inner beliefs about life in general, our fears and negative feelings in other aspects of our lives. We need to take a look at our beliefs and convictions that we have from long ago, but maybe already forgot about, or maybe, we think that they are not important for this topic of wealth. You have to go broader and deeper than what is seen on the surface.

Remember, things that we believe in, we create. We need to get rid of jealousy, hate, irritation and different kinds of fears. Some people have fear of the dark, fear of death, fear of the airplanes.

Some people have fearful thoughts that poison their life, and make it difficult to enjoy the beautiful moment of now. Sometimes people have feelings of guilt; they cannot forgive themselves and others. Some people have regrets about the past. Others were deeply hurt by their loved ones and they cannot let go and forget that painful experience. Unfortunately, this list can be very long. All of us know our own feelings. You know your own feelings and your own things that bother you, that make you feel bad, that take your attention away from your goal and the beauty of this life. So, if you are working on a particular aspect of your life, and you want to create and attract, for example, wealth, it is very helpful to pay attention and work on other negative beliefs and convictions that you might have. This will remove more blocks, will set you free, will make you happier and will help you achieve your desired results faster.

The problems that we have are the indicators of our negative thoughts, feelings and beliefs, deeply seated in our subconsciousness, that govern our life. You already know that what we believe, think about, and feel, we attract. So, it does not matter what thought makes you feel bad, whether it is about wealth or about something else, it is a negative thought that you need to eliminate.

We need to get rid of false beliefs, which are based on the idea that there is more than one power in the world. There is only one power and it is the Power of God. God is the only power that exists. We have to get rid of superstitions and eliminate our own fearful thoughts. Different kinds of superstitions, fads and fearful thoughts really poison the lives of many people, while these are only false beliefs. God is the only power and wisdom that exists, there is nothing else. His love and protection is always with us. We need to realize it, believe it, and let everything else go. God is the only power that exists. He has no beginning and no end, He was not born, so He can never die, He is the infinite, unlimited, Almighty Life full of love. There is a part of the Divine in us, in each of us; therefore, we should not be afraid of anything. Life is an infinite process; it is full of beauty, abundance, prosperity and love. When you realize it, when you let go of prejudices, when you feel connected to the Source, when you trust the Creator, when you know that His power is within you, when you know that God is always with you and that He is leading you and protecting you in all your ways, indescribable peace, calmness, love, happiness, and bliss fill your soul, your mind and your entire being. You become invulnerable, you are surrounded and led by the Almighty love, you are filled by this love and everything becomes possible in the Divine perfect order.

All the problems that we experience are attracted by our negative beliefs, thoughts and feelings. False beliefs, prejudices and superstitions take a lot of creative energy away. They make people worry, they make people feel frightened and live with expectancy of something bad. They make people think about bad outcomes and how to prevent something bad from happening. These negative false beliefs make people focus on the opposite from what they want, on negative things and ideas. They make people feel bad. And guess what can we create, if we are governed by these prejudices and false beliefs? Correct, whatever we believe, think and feel, we attract. Let go of these false negative beliefs. There is no sense in worrying about something that is not true. Just think about this. Long time ago, our ancient ancestors were afraid of lightning or thunder. They were afraid of things they did not know, could not explain and had false beliefs about. They created different fables, which tried to give some explanations to things they were afraid of, and they believed in those fables. But there is no sense in believing in something that is not true, in something that disturbs you and that doesn't serve you, in something that actually gives you the opposite result from what you want.

Therefore, it is really important to educate yourself, to surround yourself with Divine Truths, to self-improve, and it is really important to change the false beliefs, which poison the life and block you from ease, happiness and beauty of the existence. Get rid of prejudices, get rid of superstitions. Educate yourself, work on your personal growth, let go of far-fetched fears, which are not true. Don't give them your attention, don't give them the power. Stay connected to the only power that exists, the Almighty Power of God. Feel the Divine Power in you, and those shadows of false beliefs and false fears will vanish and disappear from your life completely. Free yourself from this needless burden of false ideas and beliefs. Let them go and you will free yourself from the mental blocks that prevent you from opening up to your fullest potential and living a happy and abundant life. Be free, be pure. Fill yourself with the Divine Love. Realize that you are always protected and guided by the Divine. The Almighty Power of God is always by your side. Feel the Divine Power and love in you and live your dreams, because this is what we are here for.

Fill your mind with Divine Truths. Feed your brain with positive ideas. Focus on your goals and things that you want to achieve, and these positive ideas will sink into your subconscious mind. Work on yourself and you will change your inner beliefs to the ones that will help you, benefit you and serve you.

We have to go deeper than what the problem might seem from the first sight. There might be some deep-seated feelings of guilt and unhealthy obligations. It is important to feel responsible towards the people around you, but it should not be based on guilt or any negative feelings, it should have a healthy nature. Love yourself the way you are, with everything that has happened. If you don't like something (some of your actions or deeds) you can change them, and the best time to do it is now, but you should get rid of guilt, and you should feel the feelings of love and acceptance toward yourself.

Some people feel guilty towards their parents or children, or spouses. Sometimes, there is even no ground for that feeling, and maybe, sometimes, there is. Very often, people feel guilty with no reason at all. At times, people exaggerate, make up the reasons, and punish themselves with the feeling of guilt. Sometimes, people do things that they regret later and feel guilty. So, it does not matter what your situation is, the feeling of guilt does not help, and it is important to eliminate this negative feeling.

Whatever happened, already happened, let go of it. Fill yourself with peace and love. It is already in the past, don't touch the past. It is time to move on. Right now we have a completely new moment, and in this moment we create our future. From now on, you can do things differently, if you want. The feeling of guilt, does not change anything, it does not help the other person, the one towards whom you feel this feeling. It does not help you either. Negative destructive feeling cannot help, cannot heal, and cannot bring anything good. There is no sense and no point in feeling guilty. This feeling can only poison your life, your health and bring more situations and things that will make you feel this way in the future.

We are reasonable beings. It is important to realize that maybe you were wrong, and that you want to change the situation, that you learned the lesson, and from now on, you choose to be a different person and act in a different way. It is enough. There is no point in giving the energy to the negative feelings, such as guilt, in this situation. It is more constructive to focus on the solution. We all want to fix the problem, not to create more of it.

Now, you should put all your creative energy on working on yourself and becoming the person you want to be, the person who will make you feel good, who will make you smile, the person you will be proud of. You are this person; you just need to make a new choice and a new decision. You just need to see yourself in a new light, give yourself a chance, trust the Creator and follow His lead. Fill yourself with love and forgiveness and the Infinite Love of the Universe will heal all your wounds, yours and the other person's too. That's the power of love, easy and magnificent, always here by your side. The only thing you need to do is to realize and feel its presence.

Never focus on the negative feelings, never focus on the problem. You should always focus on the opposite from that, you should always focus your attention on things you want to feel or achieve. If you know that sometimes you feel guilty towards your parents, say to yourself "I am the best daughter/son." Believe in it and you will become the best daughter/son. You will accept this belief and it will manifest in your life, because our deepest inner beliefs manifest. We attract what we really believe deep in our hearts. Whatever happened already happened. It is in the past. Let go of the past. Forgive yourself and let go. Now, is now. Enjoy the moment of now and create the future you want, the future you will feel good about and do it now. Don't try to hold on to the shadows of something that does not exist anymore. The past is gone, and it is gone for good.

Let it go. There is no point in dragging a heavy, unreal burden of pain, from the situation that is long time gone. It is time to move on. Let it go. Focus on this moment and on the things you can do now. Right now plant only the seeds of love, happiness, abundance, health, goodwill, wellbeing and wealth, and you will reap the rich harvest of joy, bliss, prosperity and happiness in the future.

Do not judge anyone. Do not judge your neighbors, relatives, friends, coworkers or just strangers on the street. When we judge someone, we focus on the negative things that we see in that person. We think about those negative things, we talk about them, we see the mental pictures of those negative things, we tell our friends about them and we attract those negative things into our lives. You know, what we think about, what we focus our attention on, we attract. Therefore, it makes more sense and is more efficient to think about, feel, talk about and focus on the things that we do want to attract, and we should let go of everything else. All of us are Divine parts of the Whole. Basically, there is no other. We are the Divine beings, beloved children of God, Divine parts of the Infinite Wholeness. Wish for other what you wish for yourself. Fill yourself with love and goodwill towards yourself and others, and enjoy peace, love and happiness of the life that expresses itself in this moment. Enjoy this moment and be the best you can be right now.

So, if your goal is to become successful, to build a good career or business, become wealthy, independent and achieve your dreams, you should also pay attention to the inner beliefs, feelings and thoughts that govern other aspects of your life and to your beliefs, thoughts, feelings and perception of life in general. Our life principles, the ideas that we accept as true in our mind and deep in our heart are imprinted in our subconsciousness. These deep inner beliefs manifest, and come into existence. All aspects of our life are interconnected and they influence each other. And if we have complexes or fads about one issue, it might also affect or block the other. A lot of people believe and are terrified of things that are based on many false beliefs. These false beliefs were instilled throughout centuries. Some people are afraid of different superstitions, curses, and envy, and these fears poison their feelings, these fears influence their actions, limit them and block them from achieving their goals. We should never forget that there is only one power in the world: The infinite Almighty Power of God; the only power that exists is God. There is a part of the Divine in each and every person, and there is a Divine Power in each and every one of us. When we realize this, when we accept it as true, when it becomes part of our nature, when it becomes our deep inner belief, we are no longer governed by these false, ancient superstitions. We are governed by the love and power of the Infinite within us. We are led, guided and protected by the Divine Power in every step of our way.

Never give away (in your mind) your power. Never give (in your mind) the power to things, people, situations and circumstances that are outside of you. Always look inside, always know that you have the power in you to live the life you deserve, to achieve your goals, to become successful, wealthy, prosperous and abundant. Always know that the Almighty Power of God is with you. God always loves and protects His beloved child, you. Outside factors don't have the power over you, if you don't give them this power in your mind. Don't give away your power (in your mind).

If you believe, that your coworker's envy might prevent you from getting a raise, you are giving your power away. You believe that some person can influence your life negatively. In your mind you focus on it, you draw mental images of it. You feel the negative feelings about this situation and you try to prevent it somehow. Your worries, your fears cannot protect you. All you are doing, is focusing on negativity, and in your mind, you are giving the power in the hands' of the other person or situation. And you already know that what you think, feel and believe, you attract. Your inner beliefs manifest themselves. Therefore, always feel your power, the power of the Divine in you. Realize and feel the Power of God by your side. Realize and feel His guidance, love and protection. Know this, believe it, feel it. There is only one power in this Universe and it is the Almighty Power of God. It is always with you. Fill yourself with love, goodwill and realization of this truth. Feel the power within you, trust the Creator, feel connected to the Source. Feel protected and safe, because you are always protected by the infinite unconditional love of God. Enjoy every moment and live your life to the fullest.

No matter what you are trying to create or what you work on in your life, either it is wealth or happiness, or relationships, remember, that the deep seated beliefs, things that you believe to be true in your heart govern you, govern your behavior, your thoughts and feelings. These deep inner beliefs manifest into your reality, they manifest as your experiences. Your inner beliefs and perception of yourself and life in general, your mental images that are imprinted deep in subconsciousness and play over and over in your head, govern your life. Our perception of ourselves, the life and the world around us, our deep seated inner beliefs (things that we believe to be true deep in our hearts) influence our actions, influence the way we hold ourselves, the way we think and feel. And they determine whether we succeed or fail.

Different open or hidden fears, complexes, fads, prejudices, superstitions, anything negative that is deeply rooted in our subconsciousness, blocks us, prevents us from the best in life, from experiencing our dreams and from achieving our goals. But don't worry, if you understand it, if you realize it, you can change it.

When you realize that these fads, fears and superstitions are not real, that they are just false beliefs, suggested to us throughout centuries from the outside, just a game of our protective imagination, they will lose the "power" in your mind. You will release them, let them go and make new conscious choices, choices that you choose for yourself, choices, ideas and things that you want or like, things that benefit you and serve you.

Trust the Divine Wisdom that is in you. Trust the wisdom of the Infinite Presence. Realize and feel your connection to the Source of the infinite truth. Realize and open yourself to the love, guidance, support and protection of the Almighty Power of God, and you will feel this love, the support, the inspiration and guidance. You will feel and realize that with God's help you are the master of your life, you are the master of your mind, you have the power to change the way you think and feel, you have the power in you to achieve your goals, to become the person you want to be, and to live the life of your dreams. You have the power to do it. Feed your mind with the Divine Truths of life, self-educate yourself and self-improve. Focus on the good, positive things, on love, on the Divine Truths and ideas, on beauty, wealth, happiness, and live your dreams. You can do it. Everything is possible with the Divine Power within you and with the Almighty Power that is always by your side.

Be selective with information you receive. It can be a good idea to limit the flow of negative information to you, where it is possible. Be selective. Be selective in what you read, what you watch, what you learn about, what you think and talk about. You can avoid some flow of the negative information. You can choose what articles to read, what programs to watch and so on, but there are situations where you cannot run away from what is going on around you. We are reasonable beings; we can choose what to accept to be the truth for ourselves. We can choose our feelings, we can choose our emotional reaction to what we hear or see.

So, be selective. If you can limit something negative, do it, and if you can't, choose what to believe and how to feel about it. When you hear or see something negative, you have a choice, you can say to yourself: "this is not true for me," period. Or "I choose love, peace, stability and wealth." You don't have to accept something just because you heard or read about it. Be selective. Choose (in your mind) whatever is happy, healthy, joyous and beneficial for you. If you hear people talk about some kind of problem or disease, you have a choice, you can always say to yourself inwardly: "I choose to be happy, I choose to be healthy. I am happy, I am healthy." You always have a choice of what to think or feel towards yourself. Choose, in your mind, things and ideas that are for you. You can choose, in your mind, who you are and what you think about yourself.

Be selective in what you say. Don't say either aloud or inwardly anything bad about yourself. Attach only good, positive things to "I am..." See yourself the person you want to be, feel it now, because you already are that person. You are the Divine being; the part of the Divine is in you. All you need to do is to allow yourself to be the person you want to be, free yourself from the mask of fear, ignorance and limitation, and reveal your true nature, a nature filled with love, wisdom, and the inspiration of the Divine.

Try to avoid negative utterances. Be selective in your social life; choose the topics for your conversations wisely. Select what you say about different issues. Avoid negative conversations, or conversations that bring the feeling of resistance or resentment. Remember, what you focus on, think about and feel, you attract. All of this might sound like a hard work: "Do this, think that, don't think or say that, choose, pay attention to your feelings and thoughts, etc." But think about this, we do all of this anyways, we think, we talk, we read, we listen, we believe. Isn't it better to choose what you want, instead of accepting whatever is given to you?

Just imagine, hypothetically, you come to the restaurant, and when the waiter is ready to take your order, you just say: "Bring whatever." Can you imagine what that person might bring you if, for example, you are in a bad mood and maybe are even mean or rude to him or her? And then, as you eat the meal, you complain about why life is unfair to you and why the meal is so bad. And maybe in an even worse mood later, you go to a car dealership. As soon as you walk in the door, you start screaming at the salesperson. (Because you are in a really bad mood, you feel frightened that something bad could happen again, that someone could fool you). And after another unpleasant conversation, with that salesperson, when he asks you, "What car would you like to buy?" you answer, "Whatever — I don't care, just bring me anything." Guess what you will get? And so on. This can become a never-ending circle. The person might feel that he or she is the victim of the situation, powerless and clueless as to what is going wrong every time.

94

Thereafter, choosing might not seem such a hard work to do. It's just like ordering your favorite food or things. It is fun. It is a pleasant experience. And when you will constantly choose positive thoughts, feelings, words, topics for conversations, and things to believe in, with time, this process will become your habit. It will imprint in your subconsciousness. You will automatically choose whatever is positive, whatever is beautiful, whatever is godlike, whatever is true, whatever is love, whatever is wealth and whatever is happiness. We attract what we think about the most, what we feel and what we believe in. It makes more sense to attract what you consciously choose, than what you are given by the mass mind. Choose love, happiness, wealth, wellbeing, good health, joy, bliss, success, gratitude, peace, and live in the world full of love, happiness, wealth, wellbeing, good health, joy, bliss, success, gratitude and peace. It's your choice. It's that easy.

Try to change your old habitual patterns of thinking, eliminate thinking about negative things and bring in new, fresh ideas. Read more self-educational literature. Try to read inspirational self-improvement books for at least one hour a day, every day. Sometimes, even changing physical habits might help, but do only what you want to do, something that you always wanted to do, but left for later. Now is the perfect time to implement those ideas. I am talking about small simple things. For example, you never meditated right after waking up, but always wanted to, start doing it. You've always wanted to drink fresh juices in the morning, start doing it. You've always wanted to go for a walk every day, but never had time for it, start doing it today. You've always wanted to eat more fruit and vegetables or make salads and eat them more often, start doing it.

If you usually have a messy room, try to keep it clean, because deep inside you want it, right? Start making your bed every morning if you haven't done it ever day. If you've always wanted to take dance classes or go to a fitness club, you can do it now. Get an advice from your doctor about what activity is the healthy and right choice for you and do it. Improve and change your posture, talk to the chiropractor or a doctor, ask him or her, what is the healthy and proper posture. First of all, improving your posture can be very healthy for you; you will look more beautiful and confident. It is really interesting because such little things as changing posture can be very powerful and helpful tools. Changing your posture can be a little uncomfortable at first, because you are changing your old habit, which takes your effort and attention; but if you try to improve your posture, it is so surprising that by being more properly aligned, at least for a few hours, how the whole world seems a little different. You start to feel more confident, or even nobler. It's like a new level of self-esteem is finding itself in the deep places of your true nature. By bringing these little changes in your life, you change your habits, you don't follow the habitual patterns anymore, and very often good changes help to motivate you, renew your enthusiasm and help you change your thought process as well, especially when you consciously pay attention to what you feel and think. It is interesting to see that usually the change of one habit to a better one automatically brings other new and positive changes with it.

Another interesting thing is that when we focus on our dreams and goals, when we meditate, when we think about and feel whatever is beautiful, godlike and joyous, when we focus our attention on things we want to achieve, and on what kind of person we want to become, this process also helps us to change our old habits. And it happens automatically; it just happens. You practice this positive thinking process and one day you just feel like doing something you always wanted, but never did, or maybe you will feel that you want to do something new. And again these can be just little things like: "Oh today, I want to ride a bike or eat a proper meal, or work out, or sit straighter etc."

So our positive changes, in our mind, change the way we act, talk, feel and think; they exchange our present habits with better ones. They improve the quality of our life, and our perception of ourselves, others, the world and life. And these positive changes bring even more positive changes, and it becomes automatic, natural. It just happens. All we have to do is to make this shift from negative to positive, and when it occurs, the magic things start to happen on their own. It becomes a natural process. You just have to remember the laws of the Universe and consciously pay attention to this process and keep it up. As you work on yourself and improve, so will everything and everyone around you.

Another important thing is, don't be afraid to ask more than once. When you focus on the fast and easy completion of the task, on the positive outcome, success and achievements, you will be led and inspired to do the right actions, and all you will have to do is act, and things will just happen. Sometimes, you don't even have to do anything, they will just happen. But there are also times, when you have to be prepared to ask more than once to hear the answer you are looking for.

For example: A person moves to another country and wants to study in college. He has gathered all the information he needs, and completed all the courses (in the same college) that should help him to be able to enroll in a full-time program. He comes to Admissions and talks to the clerk about applying, but the clerk tells him that he has to complete another course before he can apply. This future student feels that something is wrong with that answer, because he already heard that he has completed everything he needs. So, the next time he comes to college, he goes to Admissions and asks the same question again. A different clerk is there this time, and that clerk looks at his case and gives him a different answer. This clerk tells the future student that he has met all the requirements and should fill out and submit the application form. The next day this happy future student comes to Admissions again to submit the application, but he is told by the third clerk, who is on duty this time, that he is too young to enroll, and because of his age he should wait until next year to apply. This determined student feels that something is wrong with that answer again, and in half an hour he comes back to Admissions and talks to another clerk, who tells him: "You know what, let's try. Don't listen to anybody, just apply." The Admissions clerk collects from the future student all the necessary documents for him to enroll. And within a month, this happy student receives a Letter of Admission from the college, congratulating him on a successful enrollment. The student's time, effort, determination, and persistence resulted in success, in the achievement of his goal. By the way, this is a true story — it happened to the friend of mine. And keep in mind that we are talking here about such an easy and simple thing as enrollment; nevertheless, it required the student's determination and persistence.

Situations like this happen very often in different aspects of life, at work or in business. Very often people give up after the first time they hear "no". What would have happened, if this student gave up after the first rejection?

It does not mean that you have to go everywhere and bother everyone with the same question over and over again in order to get something you want. Sometimes, we need to accept some kind of rejections, and usually they are only for better anyways. What this example shows, is that when you have a clear vision of your goal, when you feel that this is the right thing to do, and this is a good and positive thing, which will bring good to you and others, which will serve the humanity, and you know that this is what you really want, you have to be determined. You have to be persistent. Don't give up easily. Don't be frustrated with the time delay. Just do it. And when you feel that it is the right thing to do, when you feel the inner urge to do it, do it. And don't be afraid of rejections. Don't be afraid to hear "no". If you knock on the door for some period of time, someone eventually will open the door for you.

> *"Ask, and it will be given you; search, and you will find; knock, and the door will be opened for you. For everyone who asks receives, and everyone who searches finds, and for everyone who knocks, the door will be opened."* (Matthew 7:7-8)

Be determined, be persistent. Focus your thoughts on your goals, on success and beauty of the life. Be thankful, see the clear vision of your dream. Know that you deserve it. Know that you have the Divine Power within you to make it. Know that the Almighty Power of God is always with you. Trust the Divine. Trust that God will lead you to whatever is perfect and right for you. Believe that you already have what you desire. Believe it to the point of conviction. Feel the anticipation, expect it, and trust. Fill yourself with calmness, gratitude and love of the answered prayer, and open yourself to the unlimited riches of the Universe. They are already here for you. They are already yours. Just open yourself, allow yourself to have it, and receive it with love, trust, calmness and gratitude.

XI

TRUE WEALTH, TRUE ABUNDANCE, TRUE HAPPINESS

The theme of this book is wealth — physical and material wealth, as well as wealth in all its aspects and all its manifestations. You have to ask yourself what is your ultimate goal, and it is happiness and success in all aspects of your life. True? We want to be wealthy and have money in order to do good interesting things, buy new nice stuff, help people, spend more time doing what we love to do, enjoy things we like, spend time with our family, etc. So, we are searching for means that can make our life more fulfilling, meaningful and happy in all its aspects.

There are many rich people who are unhappy, they are not successful in relationships, their family gives them a lot of pain, or maybe they don't even have any family. There are people who have amazing families but they have nothing to feed them with. They don't have enough money for anything. They cannot afford to buy anything good for the people they love, pay for their children's education, bring their family on vacation and even spend time with them. There are many successful professionals who are not happy in their social and personal lives, or who don't have real love; they cannot find their soul mates, and so they either live alone or with someone who is not even closely a perfect match for them. There are people who make money, but they are very unhappy at their workplace; they don't like what they are doing, their profession.

This list can be very long and time consuming. So, it is obvious that what we really want is happiness, wealth and abundance in all aspects of our life. This is real wealth, this is real abundance. All aspects of our life are interconnected, and all of them are important. That's why, very often, when people work on one issue, they can improve the other automatically. Sometimes we focus on one aspect of our life, we self-educate ourselves and we get positive results in the different aspect. For example, sometimes, the person works on wealth, he takes seminars, reads books, meditates and as a result, his social life improves, he meets new interesting people, makes new connections, or maybe loses weight. This person did not even concentrate too much on those issues; the issues just kind of automatically fixed themselves.

Sometimes people focus on relationships, they want to meet their soul mate or improve the existing relationships, and as a result, they get a raise at work or get a new and better job, or a better opportunity for business, and wealth starts to come in their life. As soon as we start aligning ourselves with the life principles of the Universe, when we focus on positive, godlike ideas, things and actions, when we feel good, when we fill ourselves with love and gratitude, focus our thoughts on our dreams, these new ideas, new ways of thinking sink into our subconscious mind. Our inner beliefs, deep-seated in our hearts, change and there is no more space for the old blocks that prevent us from achieving wealth and abundance in all aspects of our lives. These old blocks vanish, and we open to the beautiful gifts that have been waiting for us all along. Now we are ready to receive them, we are open to them and they start coming in our life, sometimes unexpected, surprising and unpredictable, but always good, and very often, even better than we could ever imagine. We know how we want to feel, we focus on it and the Infinite All-knowing Presence supplies us with the best outcome possible, because no one knows better than the all-wise Intelligence that created us. So, you know how you want to feel and God knows exactly what will make you feel this way or even better. Therefore, trust Him. Do your part by focusing on the thoughts and feelings of beauty, love, happiness, wealth, abundance, joy, bliss and success, believe to the point when you are convinced, that what you want is already yours. Feel the peace and calmness of an answered prayer. Fill yourself with love and gratitude, and open yourself to the unlimited riches of the Universe, and receive the gifts that are far beyond your most delightful and cherished dreams.

Another important thing in the process of materialization of our dreams is to completely forgive yourself and others. Feelings of hate and resentment, pain and anger can be very destructive, and can serve as pretty heavy blocks, that prevent us from achieving what we desire. Therefore, we should forgive everything and everyone including ourselves.

Forgive yourself. Remember that you are the most important person to you in this life. God always forgives us. He loves us unconditionally; He always loves and forgives you. Of course you should forgive yourself. The past is in the past; let it stay in the past. Don't bring it to the present and to the future. Don't drag something that is already gone to this moment. Let it go. Today you have a chance to create new experiences, to choose new things. It is good that you realized your mistakes, they taught you a good lesson, but it is time to let them go. Leave past to the past, concentrate on the present and put all your creative energy into things that are good, things that are beautiful, godlike, true, and create the future you desire and deserve. Stop dragging something that does not exist anymore. All we have is now. All we have is this moment of now, the present moment. Live it, enjoy it, and choose what you want. Forgive yourself, forgive yourself completely. Say to yourself:

"I love you (say your name). I forgive you (say your name). I love you dear (say your name). I forgive you completely dear (say your name). I let go of the past. I release it, and set it free. My past is perfect, my future is blessed, my present is Divine. I forgive myself and let go of all the pain and negativity. I am free, I am clean, clear and

pure. I am a wonderful person. I am the Divine being. I am the beloved child of God. God's love fills my mind, my soul and my body. God's love heals me. God's wisdom, love and forgiveness fill my entire being. I am forgiven. Thank You. I love You. I forgive myself. I love myself."

Forgive yourself, be free from the past, let it go, enjoy this moment and the love of the Divine will heal all the pain, and will set you free, to the life of happiness, health, bliss, joy and abundance.

Forgive other people. Whatever happened already happened, so let it go. There is no sense in filling sorrow or pain for something that is long time gone. This burning feeling of hate and resentment does not do anything good. You know, that what we feel and what we think about, we attract. What good can you attract by focusing on the feelings of anger, hate or resentment? God always forgives us. He loves all His children unconditionally and He always forgives us. Of course, you should forgive everybody, set them free, set yourself free of those painful, negative, pointless feelings that take away your creative energy and block you from achieving your goals. There is a part of the Divine in each and every one of us. We are the Divine parts of the Infinite Whole. There is a Divine Presence in each person. When you think about the person, see this Divine Presence in him. When you look at the person, see the presence of God in him, see his Divine nature. You don't have to become close friends with people you don't want to, but you should not feel anything negative towards them. You should completely eliminate this burning feeling of hate, anger, resentment or anything negative you feel towards others. When you think about the person, when you see that person, there should be no sting inside of you. Your feelings should be calm and neutral. Feel love and mentally send the Divine Love to the presence of God within that person. Forgive everybody. See the Divine being in each and every person, look beyond the surface. Just say inwardly:

"I forgive you dear (say the name of that person). I forgive you for everything that has happened, for everything you have done, for everything you have said my dear (say the name of that person). I know that there is a Presence of the Divine in you. I love the Divine Presence within you. I love the presence of God within you. I love you. I completely forgive you. I let go of the past. I let you go my dear (say the name of the person). I set you, my dear (say the name of that person), the past situation, and myself free. I let go and let God heal this situation, heal you and heal me. The healing presence of God is within me, it heals me completely. The healing love of God fills my mind, my soul and my body. I am healed, I am free, I

*am happy, I am blissful, I am joyous, I am
wealthy, I am successful, I am abundant, I
am happy."*

Say to the Divine:

"Thank You."

Forgive everyone, forgive yourself, let go of the past. Free yourself from this needless, pointless burden of something that does not exist anymore. Concentrate all your thoughts, feelings, and creative energy on the things that are good, beautiful, abundant, joyous; on the things that you desire; on your dreams. And what you pay all your attention to, what is on your mind throughout all day, and what you feel the most often, will be attracted to you. Eliminate negativity. Focus on what is positive, what is true, what is godlike. Concentrate on your dreams and goals. Align yourself with the Divine Truth, love and unlimited abundance. Open yourself to the bountiful gifts that are already waiting for you. Allow yourself to be happy, abundant, wealthy, successful and joyous, and Universe will help you in all your sincere beginnings.

It is important to understand, that wealth is a lifestyle. It's not just money in your pocket, it's how you feel, how you feel about yourself and everything that surrounds you, how you feel about the world around you, how you perceive life. It is a lifestyle. It is the way you think about yourself, the way you see yourself, the way you walk, talk, eat, smile, communicate with people, the way you feel while you are one on one with yourself, or when you are in public, the way you hold yourself, and the way you think and feel about your position in life, or about your sense of belonging to one or another group or class. And the most importantly it is your inner thoughts and feelings about yourself, others and life in general.

We are the Divine beings, the beloved children of God. The part of the Divine is in each and every one of us. We are already wealthy. We were born wealthy. Everything that is, is for us. Wealth is all around us: Look at the sky, it is for you; the stars, the air, the sun, the birds, the ocean are for you. Prosperity is all around you; just open your eyes and feel it. Everything you've ever wanted to become is in you, it is in your potential. You are given the gift of choice and the power of the Divine that is in you can make it happen, easily and quickly, right away, because everything, every possibility already exists in the infinite Universe. It is already yours, it is here, it is all for you, you just have to take it, open yourself, see it, feel it, realize it, believe it, live it. You already are perfect. You are the Divine being living in the perfect Universe of unlimited potential, possibilities and prosperity. You already are everything you've ever wanted to be. There is a part of the Divine in you. You already are a prince or a princess; you just need to believe in it, to open to the truth of acceptance, and to believe in your true nature. There is a Divine Power within you. The Almighty Power and unlimited unconditional Love of God are always with you. You already are in the world created for you. You already are at home, you just have to realize it, believe it, feel it. Say to yourself:

> *"I am the beloved child of God. His Divine love and protection are always with me. The power of the Divine is in me. The Almighty Power of God is with me. All the riches of the Universe are for me. They are all around me. They are already mine, they have always been mine. Now I realize it, now I believe it, now I am thankful for it. Now I accept it, now I live it. I am the beloved child of God and I enjoy His generous and unlimited gifts now and always."*

Say to the Divine:

> *"Thank You, I love You."*

Feel that now you are living this lifestyle of unlimited wealth of the Universe. Straighten your shoulders, change your posture to that of a successful, relaxed, happy, proud individual. Feel that you are worth all the best in life, that you are filled with the love and power of the Divine, feel that you have the Almighty's support. Feel the gratitude for everything that exists and let this feeling to be shown in each of your movement, when you walk, when you sit, when you eat, when you talk. And here, I am talking about healthy, loving, godlike feelings of self-esteem, and feeling that you live in the bountiful

Universe, that you are the beloved child of God, that God's love, support, guidance and protection are always with you, and that everything you want already exists, and you are always surrounded by unlimited unconditional love and unlimited riches that cannot be described with the words of the human language. Feel the healthy feeling of self-respect, pride, and love towards everything that is. Feel that you are the beloved child of God, that you are surrounded by love, beauty and immense, indescribable abundance of the Universe. Feel it, it has to be felt and seen in every word of yours, in your every move, in your every action, in your every thought, in your every step. Each moment of every day should be filled with this feeling of unlimited love and abundance of everything, abundance in every aspect of your existence, because it already is so. You just have to believe it. You just have to feel it. You just have to open to it, allow yourself to have it, let yourself enjoy it, realize it, feel it, accept it, live it, be it. Feel successful, gifted, amazing, beautiful, gorgeous, abundant, because you are. You are the beloved child of the Divine. You are perfect. Realize it, feel it, believe it, accept it. You are the perfect Divine creation, you are the beloved child of God, you are amazing. You live in the bountiful, abundant Universe; everything you've ever wanted and everything you'll ever need is already here, it is here for you. Realize it, feel it, believe it, accept it.

Feel easy and relaxed, be calm. Feel the feeling of ease and relaxation in every move, when you walk, when you watch TV, when you sit in the restaurant, when you read the book, when you talk with your spouse or friends, with your boss, with the business partner or with your parents. Even when you work, straighten your posture, feel and look proud to be who you are. You are the Divine being, the perfect creation, the beloved child of God. The success of the Universe is with you. The love of the Divine is with you. His Almighty Power is with you. There is no limit to love, beauty and abundance of the Universe.

Realize and feel the feeling of self-worth, self-esteem and healthy pride towards yourself. You are full of amazing ideas, you are talented, you are beautiful, you are love and you are loved. You are filled with the beauty, love, gratitude and abundance of the Divine. Realize it, believe it, feel it, accept it. Feel it, live it. Let it be felt and shown in each and every of your movement, in every gesture, in every smile. Feel this unlimited wealth of the Universe all around you. Feel that it is for you. Feel that you are the beloved child of God. Feel that His unlimited love surrounds you and fills you. Feel the beauty of life, enjoy every second of it, it is truly amazing. Love everyone and everything around you, love yourself. Radiate love and happiness of the successful, beloved, abundant, healthy and happy person and the magic of life will unfold in every aspect of your life.

Look at the nature, go to the park and look at the trees, lakes, streams, the sky, everything is so harmonious, peaceful and calm. Even when there is a storm or a strong wind, or huge waves in the ocean, it is always replaced by the peacefulness and calmness in a very short time. We need to learn to release the stress and tension. Of course, we are human beings and it is normal to go through ups and downs, life is always fluctuating. So, it is important to learn to let go, to relax and release stress and negative emotions. Don't allow bad feelings and everyday stress to pile up and take over. Mediation helps to relax. Reading a good, positive book, watching a good comedy with people you love can also be nice and relaxing. Reading inspirational and personal growth books is a useful practice that can calm you and put you in the positive state of mind. Go for a walk, go to the nearest park. Observe the nature, feel it. Fill yourself with its peace, love and calmness. Go to the lake or the sea, or the ocean, or the forest, if you live near one. Watch the waves, listen to the songs of birds in the morning, breathe the fresh air. Observe the rain. Listen to the nice melody it plays on the window. Enjoy the sunshine. Feel the beauty, peace and calmness of the nature. Learn from it. Each storm is shortly replaced by a beautiful calm day. When animals or birds fight, they forget about it right away, they don't go thinking about it for a month, feeling guilty, afraid, sad, or angry. They release the negative energy, as soon as the fight is over. We need to learn to release the stress right away, let the situation go, let the negative thoughts go, free ourselves from the heavy burden of self-pity, fear, guilt, anger, hate, misery, pain, regret and sadness. Release all the negativity. Let it go.

Spend more time in the nature. You can go on vacation to a beautiful quite place, or you can simply go for a walk in the park near your house, go to the shore, sit outside, read a good, positive book, spend time with people you love, and relax. Fill yourself with love, peace and calmness. Don't worry about anything. Worrying does not help to fix or solve anything; it just brings more negative energy to your life. Trust the Divine. Trust God. Feel His endless, unlimited, unconditional Love, which is with you all the time. God loves, protects, leads and supports you. His healing Love is with you. His Almighty Power is with you all the time. You are the beloved child of God. He takes care of you. Every problem will be solved in the Divine Order if you believe so. Trust the Creator. Fill yourself with love, peace, happiness and joy, and rejoice every moment of this sacred life.

Harmony, balance, gratitude, peace and love are the main principles of life. Love is the living principle of everything. God's love is in everything that is. We should align with this endless ocean of love of the Universe, and fill all aspects of our life with love. God loves you. Fill yourself with His Divine Love. Feel the feelings of love towards yourself and everything around you. Be thankful for everything you have had, and for everything you have right now. Be the part of this endless, unconditional Divine Love of God. Radiate love and goodwill all around you; radiate it on everyone around you. Be filled with this Divine Love. Love yourself. Love the world around you. Love everyone and everything with this warm, calm, joyous, peaceful and blissful feeling of the Divine Love. See and feel the presence of God in you, in everyone and everything around you. Cover yourself with the Divine Love, surround yourself with it. Radiate the feelings of love towards everyone and everything that exists and you will be surprised how beautiful this life can be, how beautiful it really is.

Say to yourself:

> *"I love you my dear (say your name). I am filled with the Divine Love of God. I feel the love, I live the love, I am the love. God loves me. I accept myself. I love myself the way I am. I am Divinely perfect. I love you my dear (say your name)."*

Say to the world:

> *"I love you. I see Divine Presence in everyone and everything. The world is always friendly and supportive towards me. The world gives me its love and I radiate my love towards the world and everything that exists. I am filled with the Divine Love of God and I radiate this love everywhere I go. I love myself, I love the world. I love everything that exists."*

Say to the Divine:

> *"I love You. Thank You for everything. Thank You."*

Don't worry about anything, don't be over-excited about anything. Fill yourself with indestructible peace of the Universe.

Say to yourself:

> *"The endless ocean of God's love and peace fills my mind, my soul, my body. The endless ocean of the Divine Love, calmness and peace fills me completely. I am the Divine being, the perfect creation, I am the beloved child of God. God loves me. He takes care of me, protects me, He supports me and leads me to whatever is perfect and right for me. His love and peace are always with me. I am filled with God's love, peace and bliss."*

Say to the Divine:

> *"Thank You."*

True happiness, the same as everything that is true, does not depend on anything. It is whole and complete entity. Therefore, our aim is to be happy just because we exist, just because we are. Do not depend on anything or anybody else for your happiness. In order to do so, we should not be attached to the result. Our happiness and satisfaction should not depend on the result or the outcome. Our happiness, joy, love and gratitude are inside of us, they are in us. We are complete Divine beings. We don't need to have the constant proof from the outside, that we are successful. We already are successful, we were born this way, nothing can take it away from us. The true happiness is really, truly and only inside of us, and it does not depend on anything or anybody else. The true happiness is in you. Feel love, happiness, peace, calmness inside of you. Self-improve, work on yourself, trust the Divine and fill yourself with love, peace and happiness.

Don't be desperate. This concept is interesting and a little difficult to explain with words. For sure, in order to understand what you want to have or achieve, you need to realize that you want this particular thing or experience. That's the first step. What is important here is that this feeling of want should be an easy, bright, calm and maybe a little exiting feeling at first (when you realize your desire), but then it should change (almost right away) to the calm, peaceful and happy feeling of the answered prayer. You don't have to walk around desperately wanting something or being over-exited (to the point of being slightly nervous about it). As soon as you understand and realize that you like something, and you want it, let go. Let it go with the feeling of ease, calmness and happiness of the answered prayer, the feeling that you feel when you already have the thing you want.

You cannot really want or need something that you already have. You cannot want something that is already yours. It does not make any sense. So, as soon as you feel that you want something, the idea of that thing can stay with you, but not the desperate feeling, not the feeling of "I want it, want it and want it!" You can keep the slight idea of the thing you like in your thoughts, but let go of the result. Let go of this thing. Feel peace, gratitude, calmness, love, satisfaction and happiness, feel that your prayer is already answered, feel it right away.

When our conscious mind, the idea in our conscious mind about something we want, and our subconscious mind, the deep beliefs and feelings about it in our soul, agree and align with each other, the result is manifested into a physical reality. You cannot want what you already have. By feeling desperate, we show that we don't believe that it can manifest. We show that deep inside we feel the lack of it. You concentrate on and feel the lack of the thing you want, otherwise you would not feel so desperate, because you cannot be desperate, you cannot need or want something you already have. And you already have all the riches of the Universe. They are here. All you need to do is to open up to them, believe and feel that it is real, that it is here, that it is for you.

Be patient. Life is a process. Sometimes, when we focus too much on the results, we forget to enjoy the process. Enjoy your life, every minute and every second of it is sacred, it is magical, beautiful, and very special. Enjoy every second of your life, bless and enjoy every experience you have. Very often it takes some time before you get the result. Sometimes you can get it right away, but very often there is a time delay before your desire gets manifested into the reality. Be patient, don't get frustrated. Don't say something like: "No matter what I do it does not work." Don't get angry or frustrated with yourself, don't get nervous, don't worry about anything. Trust the Creator and know that when the mind is ready, you will see the result. God knows what you want. He knows what you need. He is always by your side. There is always a perfect time for everything, and you will get what is perfect and right for you, in the Divine Order. Be patient. Each change might take time, and very often, the process is as valuable as the result, or maybe even more.

Don't be attached to the result. Don't let your happiness depend on the result or on the outcome of something. Do not let your happiness depend on anybody or anything outside of you. Enjoy this life, enjoy the process, enjoy every second, every moment of it. Now is the moment, now is when you feel the life, you feel the air, you move, you breathe, you live. Now is the time when you can smile or cry, it is your choice, but feel it, live it, do it now. Feel this moment of now, enjoy it. We are always in this infinite moment of now. The past is in our memory, and the future is happening every moment of now, we are always in now.

Don't worry about the past. It is long time gone. It does not exist anymore. Let it go. Forgive yourself and everybody else, and let go of the past. Don't worry about the future. You are creating your future right in this moment, with your thoughts, feelings and beliefs. God is by your side. His Almighty Power is with you. He always takes care of you, protects you, saves you, loves you, leads you to whatever is perfect and right for you. Be calm and peaceful. Fill yourself with the love of the Divine and watch the life unfold its beauty, wealth and happiness in front of you.

The future is the future; it will come in its Divine Order. The results will manifest when the time is right. Nothing matters but now. The past and the future live in our heads, and we live in the present, we are here, we are in the now. Life is an ongoing process of now. Love it, enjoy it, live it, be it. Life is happening right in front of your eyes, now. The most amazing things happen now. You can feel happy or sad, it is your choice and you make it now. Feel it, realize it, enjoy it.

True happiness is inside of you. It does not depend on anybody or anything else, it is free of the outside factors, it is your choice. Enjoy this life now, feel happy now, don't leave it for later. Don't attach happiness to some things that have to happen first. Some people say: "I'll be happy when I make enough money, when I get the new job, when I buy a car, when I open my own business, when I meet my soul mate, when I get married, when I have kids, when kids go to college, when they graduate, when they get married, when I retire, when I have my grandchildren, when I go on vacation, when the Saturday comes, when I buy that dress, when I see my friend, when I lose some weight, when my spouse pays more attention to me, when I find new friends, when the rain stops," and so on. This list is endless, because as soon as you achieve something, as soon as you reach your goal, you move on, and you want to achieve the new heights, you want to achieve even more. You will always have goals, desires and aims. It is normal.

The life expresses itself through you and it is a never ending process. Your goals and desires make you improve yourself, educate yourself, express your talents, unfold your potential, and it is great. The important thing to understand here is that we need to enjoy this moment, and we need to be happy and enjoy the process. The results come and go, they change, and sometimes what seemed amazing and fantastic 20 years ago, does not seem so fantastic any more, and it is normal. We change, our goals and desires change. We will change, and they will change with us. They grow as we grow, they change as we change. What we always have is now, this is the life, it is happening right now.

The process is an important part of life. It is good to have goals, but it is important to enjoy the process, and enjoy the moment of now, to be happy now. Not because you received something, or someone is by your side, or you are somewhere, or doing something, but because you exist, because you are, because this moment is. You are here, live your life, love it, feel this moment, be happy and do this right now.

While you are planning and visioning your goals, working on and achieving your desires, and moving towards the new heights, feel calm and peaceful. Relax, let go of all worries. Be patient and satisfied. Fill yourself with love, peace and calmness of the Divine. Relax and be happy now, not because of someone or something else outside of you, but because you exist, because you are and because you are here. Enjoy this moment of now. Be happy now. Feel this moment with your skin, with all your senses. Feel it, live it, love it. The life is happening in the infinite moment of now, don't leave happiness for later. Don't depend it on anyone or anything outside of you.

The true happiness, the true peace, the true love, the true wealth, the true gratitude, the true joy are inside of you. You already are everything you want to be, all you need is to realize it and believe it. Trust the Divine in you. Trust God. He loves you, He always takes care of you. He supports you, protects you, He leads you to the experiences and things that are perfect and right for you, to your perfect life. Everything is happening in the Divine Order. Be brave in God. Trust God. Feel His love, His power and His happiness inside of you. Feel His unconditional Love, His Almighty Power, and His unlimited Joy and Happiness all around you. God is always with you. He loves you. You are His beloved child, and you are always safe in His caring arms. Live this moment, feel it. Be happy right now. Enjoy your life and be happy right here, right in this moment.

The true peace and happiness are inside of you. They are complete, they are whole, when you feel your connection to the Source, when you know who you are, and Who is with you every moment of the existence. Then you realize that this never-ending moment of now is all we have. And now is the time to be who we truly are, and to live our life the way we want and deserve. Now is the time to let go and feel the connection with the Divine. Now is the time to feel our true nature and enjoy every second of our existence. Fill yourself with love, peace, calmness, joy and happiness of the Divine. Feel and live the moment of now with ease, trust, love, gratitude, peace, calmness and joy that are inside of you. Rejoice this moment of now and live it to the fullest.

True happiness, true love, true wealth, true peace, true joy are inside of us. They do not depend on anybody or anything else. They do not depend on any outside factor. The outside world does not have the power over your inside world, unless you let it (unless you think and believe that something outside of you, events, circumstances, people, superstitions, can influence your life or have a power over you), unless you give your power away in your mind. We are the Divine beings; the part of the Divine is in us. The power of the Divine is within us. God's Almighty Power and Love are always with us. When we realize this, when we realize and feel the connection to the Source, when we feel our connection to the Divine, we start to feel our completeness and wholeness. Nothing from the outside can disturb us; nothing can distract us from our path.

Everything you have ever wanted is here, everything you will ever need is here, it already exists. All the true notions are independent of anything outside of you. The true love, the true happiness, the true wealth, the true peace, the true harmony, the true joy are inside of you. It's your state of mind, it's your inner beliefs, it's your lifestyle, it's your perception of yourself and the world around you. It's in your feelings, it's in your being. You have to realize it and make a choice. Choose what you want to experience. Choose how you want to feel. Choose your focus. Feel it inside to be true for yourself. Believe in it. Let go of any worries or negativity, let go of the result. Realize and feel the connection to the Divine. Trust God, and rejoice living life in absolute peace and happiness, knowing that your prayer is already answered. The true happiness, the true love, the true wealth and joy are inside of us, all we need to do is to realize it, choose it, feel it and believe it. Let the Divine Power in you work miracles in your life. The constant support of God is always with you. You are always surrounded by His unlimited unconditional love and protection. Trust the Divine. Enjoy this moment. Fill yourself with love, peace, calmness and gratitude. Open to the beauty, happiness and wealth of the Universe, and its unlimited riches will flow into your life easily, naturally, effortlessly and endlessly.

XII

THE TRUE SEARCH OF THE SOUL

U nderneath it all, underneath all our goals, plans, ideas, desires and aims there is a quiet, sometimes almost invisible search for something more than we can even describe with the words. Deep inside, when you stay one on one with yourself and listen to your inner thirst, this thirst is beyond any material thing, it is even beyond happiness (in our earthly understanding, happiness that material things can bring), successful personal life and career. Some people don't even feel it, at least they think so. So, they don't even think about it, at least for now. Some people will realize it, but maybe a bit later in their life. But we all feel it on the deeper level; we all feel this thirst when we really listen to ourselves. Very often, we just don't listen to our quiet inner needs. We ignore them, and then, people are surprised why they feel dissatisfied, empty, nervous and disturbed. Even if they are wealthy and achieved many of their goals, they still feel the lack of something. Even though, they kind of have everything, something is missing.

Some people try to shut this inner thirst by alcohol or by some worldly pleasures, by greed, or achieving even more "medals", or making even more money. They try to find it in worldly relationships looking for the source of love, but still feel unsatisfied, even if they find a romance, a soul mate, a good friendship or understanding of others. We all long for something more, for something deeper, for something more meaningful, for something more fulfilling, and it is our awareness of who we are, the awareness of our true nature, the realization that we are the Divine beings and that there is a part of the Divine in us, there is the Divine Power within us, Divine Love, Divine Wisdom. We all long for the connection with the Source, connection with the Divine, feeling oneness with God's Presence in us, feeling oneness with God. We are thirsty for the Divine knowledge, for self-improvement, for learning the laws of the mind and the laws of the Universe. We are all thirsty for this Divine knowledge that can show us who we really are, how we can improve ourselves, what is our real potential and how we can implement it all, in our never ending way forward, higher, to our higher levels of being, to God. We are in our constant search for the connection, for the oneness with the Divine, and for the knowledge that can help us in our self-development and in expressing our fullest potential, and our true nature, here and now.

Very often, even if we do realize this, even if we want to learn about the laws of the mind, even if we want to self-improve, we do it because we want to achieve something. We want to be happy, we want to meet the love of our life, we want to have a happy life and a happy family, we want to have a good career, we want to have money and wealth. We want something, and especially when we don't have it, or when we feel pain, we start looking for the answers. We start educating ourselves, read the self-improvement books, attend seminars, look for the teachers or mentors, and we start to work on ourselves. Which is pretty good. There is nothing wrong with that. As long as you self-improve and move forward that's amazing.

Very often, some circumstances lead us to where we are supposed to be and help us educate ourselves, help us improve, move forward and learn new things about ourselves and the world. Very often, pain and lack, serve as the indicators that we need to work on this or the other aspect of our life. Our positive dreams and desires are blessing from God, they motivate us, show us what to do next, make us work harder and become even better. This is all great. But what would you do, if you already got everything you've ever wanted? Would you stop moving forward, would you stop educating yourself, because you already achieved everything, you don't need to do anything in order to achieve your goal? The answer to this question can be different, either "yes", or "no", or "I don't know," but no matter what people answer to this question, and it does not even matter if they even ask themselves this question, our true inner nature will always long for this true Divine fulfillment, for this deeper meaning, for this higher state, for unlimited, unconditional, genuine love which only the connection with Divine can give, for the oneness with God.

When we understand it, when we realize it, we can make it our number one goal. We will not improve ourselves and grow spiritually in order to achieve something, but we will improve ourselves, grow spiritually, look for the ways to understand, to realize the laws of the Universe, and will seek to feel the connection to the Divine, as the goal in itself, as a number one goal. And everything else will follow, because when you put the God first, everything else just follows.

You align yourself with the universal principles of life. You act in accordance with laws that govern our Universe. You align yourself with the Divine Love, with what is true, real, endless and timeless. You become open to the never ending love and power of the Divine. You no longer block or stop the flow of beauty, love, wealth, peace, abundance and joy to your life. You know who you are. You know you are worth all the best in life. You know that everything you've ever wanted is already here, and you know it is for you. You are free from worries, struggles, and fear. You are free, peaceful and calm. You love and you trust the Divine. You feel the guidance, love and protection of God. You radiate love, wealth, happiness and goodwill. You see the Divine Presence in everything and everyone around you. You realize and feel the power, love, wisdom, peace, and happiness of the Divine inside of you. You feel the Almighty power and unlimited, unconditional love of God by your side. You align with what is real, true, beautiful and godlike. You realize that the only power that is, is the power of the Divine in you. The only power that exists is the Almighty Power of God, which is always by your side. You feel your connection to the Source, your oneness with God, and everything else just happens. You get inspired to the right actions, and the right deeds, and all the beauty, wealth and happiness of the world just flow into your life with ease. Everything just follows, it happens on its own, easily and effortlessly, like it always is, when you are ready, when your mind is ready.

Remember, we don't improve ourselves in order to achieve something easily and effortlessly (even though there is nothing wrong with that either, it just can be not as powerful as it should), we self-improve and grow spiritually, because this is the call of our soul, it is the call of our true nature, it is what we really long for. And when you do so, you find the true love, the true wealth, the true happiness, the true joy, because they are inside of you, it cannot be destructed or disturbed by any outside factors, and everything else just follows, it just happens.

When you are clear of negativity, when you realize and feel your Divine nature, when you feel your connection and oneness with the Divine, you get inspired. Of course we need to act, prepare ourselves, learn the laws of the Universe, train and discipline our thoughts and feelings, act and do something in order to achieve our goals and fulfill our plans, but when you focus your thoughts on what you want, when your feelings correspond to that thought and agree with it, when you feel the Divine Presence in you and feel the connection to the Divine, you act from inspiration. You think, make decisions and do things because you are inspired to do so.

In order to achieve something, you can prepare yourself for a while, train your body (if you are an athlete), find the right business partners, work on yourself, improve and educate yourself, work hard in the office, at your work place, and that is great. We are here to create and to succeed. It gives an amazing feeling of fulfillment, when we create something that serves humanity and brings success to ourselves. So, definitely we have to work and act, but when your mind is ready, when everything is ready, when you are ready, at the moment of triumph, at the moment of success, it is more than just simple actions. It is pure inspiration working in us. It is God's Presence working miracles in us and in our lives. It is the great feeling of ease, when God is working in you. He dances your dance, He runs your race; He closes the deal of your life; He sings your song; He expresses Himself through you. It brings great ease to you when you (the human in you: your ego, your worries, your prejudices, your fears) finally relax, let go, and completely trust the Divine within yourself, and when you completely trust God, who is always with you.

At this point you can still act, but it feels easy, free, like you are not even doing anything. You just relax, let go, trust the Divine completely, and fully open up to this inspiration, to this work of God in you. And your true nature unfolds, inspired, triumphant and full of the Divine freedom, love, ease, and triumph. It is God working inside of you. He walks and talks in you, He deals with your business partners in you, He dances your dance, he runs your race, He sings your song, He unfolds infinite possibilities and introduces you to the infinity, which riches are beyond any imagination possible. That's the moment of real triumph, of real success. We can feel it from time to time, we can live it every day, it is your choice. Every human being knows this feeling, this amazing feeling of the Divine inspiration, ease, love and freedom, when time just stops, when it feels like you fly, swimming in the Divine triumph, success and bliss. It's the time in your childhood when you won the soccer game, when you hit that ball and it flew across the whole field, right into the gates, when you hit the ball with your bit, playing baseball in your school baseball team, when you sang your favorite song and won the contest when you were 12, when you met really nice people, and spent whole day with them, but it felt like 5 minutes, when you wrote your poem, or when you were laying on the grass looking straight into the blue sky, and it felt like time just stopped, like you can be there the whole day, when it felt like you are flying in this endless, peaceful, free Divine inspiration and infinite love of the Universe. That's how we feel when we are fully open, when we feel our oneness with the Divine. We are complete, free, limitless, endless, full of love, peace, calmness, gratitude, bliss, happiness and joy.

If you say you don't remember, sometimes simple, but very precious events from the past, from your childhood when you felt this way, or you think you did not have such experiences, you still know what it is. Even if, for some reason, you don't remember it. You still know what it is. If you listen to yourself, it is in you, it is always in you. It is in your nature. No words can even closely describe it. The Divine Presence is always with you, the part of the Divine is in you. If you quiet your thoughts, if you listen to the quiet, calm and loving Presence within you, you feel it.

So, we all know what this state is. The question is, how often we realize it, how often we think about it, how often we remember about it, how often we feel it. And again, it is your choice, you can feel this unlimited love, the Divine inspiration, the Infinite Presence in you, connection and oneness with the Divine whenever you want, and even all the time. It is always there, you just have to realize it, feel it, trust it, open to it completely. And your life will gain colors you did not know that even existed.

We can live like this every day, it is your choice. Look at successful people, the way they talk, the way they act, the way they sit, the way they eat, the way they walk. They look free. You can feel this inner ease, this sense of freedom, something that is beyond the words. You feel this presence of freedom. When you talk to a successful person you feel this presence, this touch of inspiration, this openness to something that you really, really like. Even if the person is successful in only one or few aspects of his or her life, maybe only in his or her career, or in the relationships with people he or she loves, this person was able to open up to the success in this particular area of his life. He was touched by the Divine inspiration and his dreams manifested into the reality. That's why success is so attractive, that's why it looks and feels so tasty, that's why it is so magnetic, that's why when you look at it you want it, because you sense the way, to what you really long for. And what you really long for is expressing your true nature through Divine inspiration, realizing and feeling your connection and oneness with God.

When we put God first, when we improve ourselves, study and realize the laws of the Universe, when we grow spiritually, when we realize our true nature, realize and feel our connection with the Divine and when we make it a goal on its own, when we make it our main aim and goal number one, we reach the state of inner fulfillment, satisfaction, peace and joy, we align ourselves with the love of the Universe and everything else just follows, on its own. The rest, your goals, your plans, your desires, wealth, happiness, love, success, career and other riches of the world just follow, when you are ready. They come in a perfect balance. The riches flow to all aspects of your life, because that is the real, true abundance of the Universe, and you are open to it, you are ready.

When you are fulfilled the fulfillment follows. When you are blessed the blessings follow. When you are filled with trust and love, the real love follows. When you are filled with inspiration and happiness, the true happiness follows. When you are open to and filled with wealth, when you feel it, when it becomes your lifestyle deep inside of you, and in your mind, when it becomes your deep inner belief, a part of you, something you already have in you, the true wealth follows. It has no other choice, but to manifest, because you already are what you want to be, you are on the inside, so you are also on the outside. It all happens when you already feel that you have it inside of you, and it shows on the surface, it manifests into your reality when you are ready. Your inner state manifests it into the reality. You are who you are. And you already are everything you want to be. You are the Divine being, the part of the Divine is in you, and if you follow the true search of your soul, you come home, and you are reminded who you really are.

XIII

MY CHOICE IS LOVE

In our life we meet two opposite feelings love and fear. Fear is an opposite of love. Fear makes people do crazy things. Fear holds people back from achieving what they want. This feeling is a very strong block for many good things. Of course, we have to be cautious, know and understand repercussions of different things and actions. So, the amount of healthy natural "fear" is ok, like the fear of falling down or the fear of a loud noise. In the nature these natural instincts serve as warnings, and often help to save lives. So, you do need to understand and learn the laws of the Universe in order to consciously choose what to do and how to do it. For example, we know how to use fire, we are not afraid of it. When we use it according to the laws, it serves us, but it can also burn, if we do something wrong, but we are not afraid of fire. The same analogy can be made with water, or electricity, and so on. The fear that goes beyond these natural precautions is, as I call it, unhealthy fear. This comprises our worries, anxieties, and fear that we can get sick, that we can get fired, that we can lose our money, that something bad can happen, that he or she will not call tomorrow, that we can lose our business, that we fear the dark, and so on. Belief in different prejudices and superstitions also produces fear.

Fear shows up when we lack the knowledge, when we don't know, when we can't understand or explain something. Unknown can scare only when you are not willing to educate yourself, when you don't trust the Almighty Presence that created you enough, when you are not willing to look your fear in the "eyes" and say: "I know that there is a perfect Divine scientific explanation to it (even if I don't know about this yet). I trust the Divine. Everything happens in the Divine Order and Divine Will. I trust the Creator and know that He is my savior and my protection".

Throughout the history people have been afraid of unknown. This fear came out of the lack of education, and the lack of knowledge of the laws of the Universe. From this non-acquaintance, from lack of knowledge and lack of understanding of the true laws that govern the Universe come a lot of false beliefs. And one of them is a belief that there is more than one power that exists. Fear is present when we believe in more than one power that governs the Universe. This unhealthy fear enchains, petrifies and does not allow us to open to our fullest potential, doesn't allow us to hear the Divine inspiration in us, it messes with our minds.

Lose all the worries and anxieties, let go of fear, let it vanish from your life. Many things you fear are not true. They don't exist. Many situations you fear will never happen. Many problems you fear either don't exist (they are just in your imagination), will soon be happily solved or will even solve themselves, because around 70% of problems get settled on their own, even without your physical participation in it. Always remember that there is only one power that exists: The power of the infinite Almighty Presence inside of you, inside of every one of us — the Power of God. The only power that exists is God.

When you realize and believe this, prejudices, superstitions, fads, and fears disappear. They dissolve in the endless love of the Universe, the Divine Love which heals our mind and our soul. When you fill yourself with love of the Divine these fears disappear completely, they vanish. If you are filled with love, there is no space for anything else. It is your choice; it is either love or fear. Either love or fear can govern your life. Fear is a mental picture, the wrong thought, false believe, it is not real. Love is everything that is. It is the living principle of everything that exists. It is in you and in everything that is, so choose it.

In your mind you always have a choice. You can consciously choose what to think, what to feel and how to react. Your choices determine the outcome; they bring the results to life. Let go of the false beliefs, they are not true, they don't do anything good. Let go of fear, prejudices, fads and superstitions, they are not true either. They are products of the mass mind. Some of them were imposed on us through the centuries. That's why they might look real, but they are not, they are nothing more than the lack of knowledge, nothing more than false beliefs. They are not true. They don't have any power, if you don't give them the power in your mind. Choose love, it is real, it is infinite and endless. And always remember that there is only one power that exists, it is the power of the Divine in you. God is the only power that exists. Realize it, believe it, feel it. And remember you have the ability to choose. You can choose in your mind what to think, what to focus on, what to believe in, what to believe deep in your heart, and the results will follow your thoughts, your thinking and feeling pattern. You make your choice in your mind and results follow according to it.

Choose love, unlimited love of the Universe. Fill yourself with the Divine Love, fill your mind, your soul, your body with love. Feel it, live it. Feel the feelings of love and gratitude towards yourself, the whole world and God. Focus your thoughts on love, on happiness, on your goals and desires, on good and godlike things, on abundance, bliss and joy. Believe it and feel it, and you will attract it. Never criticize or condemn yourself. Realize, know and feel your true nature. You are the Divine being, the perfect creation, the beloved child of God. His love, support, guidance and protection are always with you.

Eliminate the feeling of guilt from your life. Guilt is very destructive feeling, it always leads to fear, fear of punishment. When you feel guilty, you feel like you need to be punished, or you want to punish yourself. You feel like you don't deserve something or even everything good, because you are bad. You did something and you cannot forgive yourself for that. And it makes you afraid. You are afraid of punishment. So, guilt leads to fear. And when you feel guilty and fearful at the same time, it is twice destructive. But once again you have a choice. You can always choose what to think about, what to focus on, what to believe in and what to feel.

Forgive yourself. Let go of guilt. Let go of fear. God always forgives you, He loves you. You are His beloved child. He is always by your side. His love is endless, unlimited and unconditional. Don't be afraid of anything. God is the only power that exists. And His Almighty Power and unconditional Love are always with you. He is always by your side. He leads you, protects you, supports you and takes care of you. He loves you. God always forgives you. Forgive yourself. Let go of the past actions and deeds, they are long time gone. They don't exist anymore. You are a new person now, you are different. Forgive yourself, make a new choice. What matters is right now. We live in this moment of now, and here we create our future, and we do that with our thoughts and feelings. What future are you creating? What future do you want to create? What would you like to attract? It is your choice. Choose love, freedom, joy, happiness and wealth. Focus your thoughts and feelings on love, gratitude, abundance, joy, success, triumph and you will attract it. It will manifest in your life, because Love always loves, forgives and gives. And you are dealing with the Divine Love of God, and the treasures it brings with it are beyond any description.

Fear is the main reason for procrastination; it is its true nature. The fear of failure, the fear that you will not be able to complete the task, the fear that you will not be able to do it as good as you want, the fear of not having enough talent, knowledge or ability to complete the task, the fear that even if you do complete it, it will not be as successful and it might be rejected or not appreciated, the fear of not getting what you want makes you passive, stops you, enchains you, puts you into the passive mode. It is the fear of leaving your comfort zone. And you have this fear only because you are afraid that you will fail, that you will not be able to do it, and even if you will do it, you will spend a lot of time and effort for it, but it will not be successful at the end. You are afraid that instead of the desired result you will fail and it will hurt you. You are afraid of lack of what you want. This fear makes you stop, makes you sabotage yourself, and makes you delay your tasks for an unreasonable period of time or even forever. It is important to understand, that this fear is nothing more than a false belief, than a negative perception of yourself, of your abilities and of your future. It is just needless, negative focus on lack of what you desire. And what you focus on you attract. Is this your choice? What do you want to attract? Obviously, the opposite, you want to attract what you desire. Therefore make a new choice, and make a new focus.

Fear is nothing more than a false thought, false belief coming from the lack of education, the lack of knowledge of the laws of the Universe and the lack of enough trust to the Divine. Knowing this, it is really easy to deal with procrastination. You already know that the power of the Divine is in you. The unconditional Love and the Almighty Power of God are always with you. It is the only power that exists. You are the Divine being, the beloved child of God. God loves you, He always helps you and supports you. And with His help everything is possible. All you have to do is to choose what you want, choose your focus, focus your thoughts and feelings on the successful completion of your task, and on your goal. Let go of fear. Choose and feel love, calmness, satisfaction, gratitude and happiness of the answered prayer. And trust God. He is your hope and everything you'll ever need.

God always helped you. Look back at your life, and you will see (you will feel deep inside of you) that He has always helped you. And you can be sure of that, because you are here, you're present in this moment. He has always helped you and supported you. God is helping you now, and He will always help you. All is good. You can relax, trust God, fill yourself with calmness, peace and confidence, and you can continue with your task, knowing that the Almighty support of the Divine is here, by your side. God is helping you right now at this moment. Don't delay life, don't delay your success and triumph, don't delay happiness, don't delay expression of your fullest potential. Enjoy, feel this moment of now, because now is the most precious, beautiful and perfect moment. All our existence is an endless, perfect moment of now.

Let go of fear, let go of unhealthy fear completely. Lose fear. Let it disappear from your life completely, let it vanish. Trust the Divine in you. Trust God. Open to God completely. Open to His love, to His inspiration, to His protection, to His support. Feel the Divine Presence in you, feel the power of the Divine in you. Feel the Almighty Power of God, which is always with you. Fill yourself with love, trust and gratitude. And where love is, there is no space for fear. Fear leaves, and when the fear leaves, there is nothing else left, but love, endless, unconditional, healing, infinite love of God. Out of that love comes gratitude to God, to life, to yourself, to everything that is, gratitude for everything that exists, for beauty of this moment, for feeling so good and amazing, gratitude for everything that is, gratitude for your own being and gratitude on its own, not for something, but on its own. And out of that gratitude comes even more love, immense, indescribable, infinite, unlimited, unconditional Divine love, that fills you completely, that fills the whole world around you. Radiate this love, feel it, live it, be it. Love yourself, love the Divine Presence in you, love the life, love the world, love God, love everything that is, because everything that exists is Him.

XIV

WHEN A STUDENT BECOMES A MASTER
OR
FROM KNOWLEDGE TO PRACTICE

Now is the time to transform everything you have learned to practice. There are instances when people read a lot of self-improvement books, they attend lectures and seminars, they know a lot, but when you don't use your knowledge on practice, nothing happens. What is the use of the car, if you have it in your garage, but never drive it? What is the use of knowing how to play the piano, if you never play it? Knowledge on its own is amazing, but using your knowledge in order to serve yourself and humanity is even better. You can have all the great concepts in your mind about how the laws of the Universe work. You can be educated, and you can learn a lot about the topic of positive thinking and self-improvement, about laws of the Universe and about how to use them in order to be happy, healthy, wealthy and successful, but if you do not implement your knowledge on practice, you will not see the desired results. You can be very smart, educated, very knowledgeable, which is great, but you will not see the results you want in your life, unless you use this knowledge, unless you apply these laws of the Universe on practice, in your life, in your everyday life.

The Divine knowledge and the Divine Truths should be shown in your life as manifestation of your dreams and desires. In order for this to happen the Divine ideas should be written in your heart, they should sink in your subconsciousness and be imprinted in it. It is not enough for you to just say: "I am wealthy, I am happy, I am successful," which is pretty good on its own, but in order for it to manifest in your life you have to feel it, you have to know it, you have to believe it to the point when you are convinced that it is true, that it is how it is supposed to be, that it already exists. The true beliefs of your heart, that's what matters. The deep inner beliefs of your soul, your deeper truth that you believe in, govern your life, influence what you say or do. The deeper inner beliefs, that's what manifests into the reality.

For example, let's say your goal is to be successful and wealthy. So, you read positive books, and try to change the way you think. You practice positive affirmations, you say to yourself: "I am wealthy, I am wealthy, I am successful," and you even repeat it a few times a day and you kind of even feel that you believe it. You affirm: "I am successful, I am successful, I am wealthy", but you don't see many changes or desired results and you wonder what's going on. Don't get me wrong, affirming positive ideas is a good technique for the start, but for example, if you work on creating and attracting wealth into your life, and you affirm "I am wealthy, I am successful", but at the same time, when you go to the store, when you have to buy something, or when the bills come and you have to pay them, you get that annoying feeling inside, that feeling suggesting that you don't have enough. That fear, that annoying feeling of worry that your monetary matters are not as good as you want them to be. If you have that feeling, the feeling and belief that you always fail, and can never make the ends meet, that is your inner belief, that is your dominant thought, that is your truth, that is what's imprinted in your subconsciousness, and that's what manifests in your life. That is your deep inner belief that governs your life. Don't be surprised of the results. Don't be surprised of not getting what you want, because you are vibrating an opposite of what you want. You feel the lack, therefore you send a request for the lack into the Universe and that's exactly what you get. You attract the lack of what you want.

So, what we need to do is to transform our theoretical knowledge into our practical thinking, feeling, believing, having and living it. We should implement our knowledge on practice, use it in our everyday life and live it. We should show that we know and apply the laws of the Universe. We need to show it and prove it with our results, with manifestation of our dreams and goals.

In order to change our inner beliefs, we have to be patient. Sometimes change can happen in a second, but very often it takes time. Therefore, you have to be patient and supportive to yourself. You have to always know about, feel and believe in the power of the Divine in you and in love, support and guidance of God. He is always with you, He loves you, supports and helps you all the time. Repetition of the Divine Truths, positive affirmations and positive thoughts is very helpful. When you repeat something over and over again for a while, you focus on it, you think about it and it starts sinking into your subconsciousness. Therefore, repetition of positive ideas, thoughts, affirmations and Divine Truths helps to transform our inner beliefs, our habitual thinking and feeling patterns, and our perception of ourselves and the world around us. Eliminate negativity in your mind regarding all aspects of your life, everyone and everything. See the presence of God in yourself and in everyone and everything that exists. Focus on your goals. Focus your thoughts and feelings on your dreams and your goals. Feel the presence of God inside of you, feel His power in you, feel His Love and His wisdom. Think about your goals like you already achieved them. Think about yourself and feel yourself the way you want to be, because you already are the person you want to be, you just have to realize it and believe it. Don't give the power, in your mind, to anything and anybody outside of you. Everything you'll ever need is already here, it is inside of you. You just have to realize it, open to it, believe in it, accept it, let yourself have it, let yourself experience it. The power of the Divine is in you, the Almighty Power of God is with you all the time.

Affirmations can be very helpful in the process of positive transformation of our thoughts, feelings and beliefs, as well as meditations, reading the inspirational, positive self-improvement books, listening to the inspirational audio programs, watching self-improvement video programs, attending lectures and seminars, educating yourself, disciplining your thoughts, your feelings and your reactions to the outside world, to the situations, people and events. Stay determined, stay focused on your goals. Watch your feelings, pay attention to them. Feelings are your indicators. If you feel good, you focus on what you want. If you feel bad, you have to change your thoughts, because you are focusing on the lack and limitations, on the opposite from what you desire. Trust God. Know that He loves you unconditionally. He always forgives you, He supports you, He protects you and takes care of you. He leads you to whatever is perfect and right for you. Realize your Divine nature, and know that God, His Love, His wisdom, His power, and His abundance are always within you.

Writing down the affirmations and your goals can also be very helpful and useful practice. You can make a habit of writing a 10 to 15 day goal plan, in which you can write down your goals that you will achieve in the next 10 or 15 days. You can list goals that you plan to achieve during this time period in your financial, personal, physical and spiritual aspects of your life. Take a piece of paper and note your goals for next 10 or 15 days. Write down the date on that page too. For example: "By (*date*) I will ..." and list your goals. Planning and writing down your goals help to concentrate on them. This technique will help you think about your goals more clearly, will help to make your planning more precise and it will give you a timeline. You can note a long term goal plan as well, your goals for a year or, maybe, even for the next 10 years. It can also be useful to write down the affirmations you repeat to yourself. Even if you found that affirmation in the book, write it down with your own hand and read it. Repeat and repeat it, again and again. Repetition helps you to get used to the new ideas, it helps these new ideas to sink into your subconsciousness and become your nature. That's how inner beliefs are changed; they have to become automatic, effortless, natural.

When you write down something it really helps, because first of all you write it with your own hand, then you read it, you see it and this helps you to absorb this information better. Just think about it, when you were in school, you read the book, you became familiar with it and discussed it, but then you had to write a journal entry or an essay on that book. That's how you learned the information in it. That's how your knowledge of the book was used on practice in that class, and such exercises also prepared you for your future studies. When you had to write research papers at school, college or university, you read different articles and books, you attended classes or lectures, where the teacher talked about that particular issue, then you thought about the topic of your essay, you made a plan of how to write it, you noted the points that you wanted to mention in your paper, and then you wrote the first draft, the second draft, etc. By the time you produced the final copy, the material, the knowledge really sank into your brain. And then you presented your paper to the class. At that point you knew the material, and could use it in order to teach it to other students in your class. After all these steps, you mastered the topic to some extent and that knowledge sank to the deeper levels of you consciousness.

See the similarity with what you are doing right now? You are studying the laws of the Universe, the ways of disciplining your thinking and feeling process. You are learning to consciously choose, and attract what you have chosen to your life. And you just want to read a few books and say: "Ok, I am done. Where is the result?" Throughout your entire life you used to think, feel and act without consciously choosing and disciplining your thoughts and feelings, and now you want to read 10 books and say: "Why it does not work? I am trying so hard, I want it so bad, but nothing happens. The technique is broken; it does not work for me." Sounds familiar? It is the same as back in school. You learn something first, find out about it, read about it, gather the knowledge, write it down, study it, repeat it, show how you can implement and use it in a particular situation and test it. The knowledge sinks into your subconsciousness, becomes your real knowledge, something you really know and believe in. It is the part of you now; you practice it, use it, and get the results you desire, perfect grades in the school of your life.

Be patient, stay determined. Choose what you want. Stay focused on your goal, feel good, focus your thoughts, focus on your desire. Trust the Divine. Feel the Divine Presence in you. Feel the power of the Divine in you. Feel the unconditional Love, the Almighty Power, and the unlimited support of God by your side. Affirm the Divine Truths. Be in this new state of thinking and feeling all the time, all day long. Focus on it, make this shift from negative to positive happen — the shift from one way to another, the shift to the direction you choose, to the direction you desire. Do it for the whole day, week, month, for as long as you can, for as long as it takes to implement this shift, to make it happen. Do it until you feel it, until these new Divine Truths sink into you, into your subconsciousness, until they become a part of you, become your true, deep-seated beliefs in your heart. Do it to the point when you are convinced, when you feel it with all your cells, till you live it.

Feed your brain with information that is positive, godlike, happy, abundant, healthy, and joyous. Think thoughts of happiness, wealth, prosperity, love, gratitude, joy, bliss, success and triumph. Feel it, believe it, feel every positive godlike word you affirm. Feel every happy, joyous, successful and loving thought, which is focused on your dreams and goals. Feel that all the good and positive things you say about yourself and your life are true. Feel that you are wealthy, feel that you are abundant. Know and feel that you are happy, that you are joyous, that you are healthy, that you are loved, that you are talented, beautiful and amazing. Realize and feel your true nature. You are the Divine being, the perfect creation. You are the beloved child of God. Relax and repeat to yourself (and you can affirm this either with open or closed eyes):

"I am happy! I am healthy! I am wealthy! I am abundant! I am prosperous! I am successful! I am loved! I am grateful! I am fulfilled! I am filled with the Divine Love, peace and calmness! I am wealthy! I am joyous! I am successful! I am happy! I am abundant!"

Feel it. Say to the Divine:

"Thank You!"

And enjoy the beauty, calmness, love, gratitude and satisfaction of the prayer that is already answered.

Follow your heart. In everything that you do trust the Divine Wisdom that is in you, the tiny quiet voice of the heart, that we often don't hear, pretend not to hear, or don't want to hear. When you read something, when you are suggested something, always think if it is good for you, if it is for you at all. Determine your own way, look inward, look within, pay attention to what is going on in your inner world. No one has access to that world except for you and the Divine Presence that is in you. Trust God. He created you, He knows what is perfect and right for you. And find your own way, find your path, the path that is perfect for you. Choose — choose what you are and what you are not. You always have a choice. If you hear something, if you learn something, even if it is a thought in your mind, a thought that you don't like, a negative thought, it can be a product of mass mind, so you can always say to yourself:

"This is not for me. I choose to be happy, I choose to be wealthy, I choose to be successful, I choose to be loved. I am a Divine being, I am amazing, I am beautiful, and I am filled with Divine Love and gratitude. I am happy. I love myself, I love life. I am happy and grateful."

You can always choose what is for you and what is not, what is you and what is not. Choose love, happiness, abundance, prosperity, wealth, joy, bliss, triumph and success. Believe it, feel it. Feel the calmness, gratitude, love and satisfaction of the answered prayer. Open to the riches that are here, that are for you, and you will be amazed of love, generosity and bountifulness of the Universe. And the riches that will flow endlessly into your life will be far beyond any of your expectations.

What can help you stay persistent and tune your feelings in the right direction for the successful creation process is determining your reason for your desire, determining your "why." When you set your goals, they can be something like a good career, a great salary, success, wealth, a new successful business, a new great job and so on. But it is really important to determine the "whys" of your heart, your real, true goals. For example, your general goal is to be wealthy, to have money, to be successful, and it is a great goal on its own, and it can be your dream, but is there a deeper "why" behind this goal. Why do you want to be wealthy? Maybe because you want your kids to go to a better college. Maybe you want to take your loved ones on that trip to Europe. Maybe you want to help your parents, to buy them a house, to see the smiles on their faces when you tell them that they don't have to work anymore and can enjoy their life, travel, and spend time with their grandchildren. Maybe you want to buy something nice for your wife, daughter, or son.

Sometimes the "whys" can even come from a different aspect of life and not be connected with the general goal at all. For example, a person might say: "I want to have a good career, I want to be successful, I want to make a lot of money." And one of the reasons for that is because he loves to play golf. He always wanted to play golf professionally. He wants to take lessons from the greatest golf teachers in the world, and he wants to play golf for at least five hours a day, every day. So, that's his "why." And this "why" has an emotional flavor to it. It means something to this person. It touches him deeply, it awakens feelings in him, it makes him want to do something in order to achieve this goal. There are always some "whys" that touch your deeper feelings. Some or maybe even many "whys" that mean something more to you than just general concepts of wealth and success, something that comes from the heart and you can call it a real inspired dream.

Determine your "why" or "whys." They can help you stay focused on your goal, they can motivate you, inspire you, support you in the moments when you feel that nothing works. It is normal to feel ups and downs, life has its own fluctuation, it is not constant, but it is also important to stay loyal to your choice, remember about it and stay focused on it no matter what. Your "whys" can help you activate your feelings, really feel what you affirm, visualize or focus your thoughts on when you work on manifesting your desires. It adds flavor to your goals, it adds reality, the real taste of your dreams.

For example, you want to be successful, you want to be wealthy and one of the reasons for this goal is that you want your kids to go to the best university in the country. You want to fulfill your son's dream to become a doctor. Think about it; imagine he is already attending that university. Imagine that he is happy, he enjoys it. Imagine that he graduates from that university. Imagine how everybody, your family and friends congratulate him on this achievement. Imagine that he finds an amazing job, he is a doctor now. He is happy, and you hear how his friends congratulate him, your wife and you. Feel proud and happy for him. Feel how good is to feel the taste of the answered prayer. Your dream came true, it is real, it is right here. You can feel it. You can taste it. Feel it, believe it. The whole thought of this dream coming true makes you feel good, makes you smile.

Let's take a look at another example, you want to be successful, you want to be wealthy because you want to buy a yacht. It's your dream. It is one of your "whys". Why not? Again think about it, think about your new, beautiful, amazing yacht. Visualize it, imagine you are sailing it. Imagine you are on it, feel the smell of the new yacht, feel the fresh ocean breeze on your face, feel it. Just a thought of you having this yacht now, makes you smile, it makes you feel good.

So, that's how these little and big "whys" that each of us has, can help you with activating the right feelings during the creation process. They can motivate you, keep you determined, help you to stay focused on what you want. The main idea when you think about your dreams, when you visualize your goals, your "whys" is to make sure you feel good. The feelings are the indicators of your focus. If you feel good, you are in the right direction, you are focusing on what you want. If you feel bad, you are focusing on the opposite from what you want, you are focusing on not having what you want. If you feel bad when you think about your goals and dreams, you focus on lack and limitations. That's why you feel bad. Therefore you have to change your focus, change your thoughts, beliefs and feelings, to the positive ones, to the ones that focus on having what you want.

Another important idea is to release your attachment to the result. The attachment to something is nothing more than focusing on lack of that thing. Think about this, if you already have something, if you know that you will always have it and nothing will ever happen to this thing, that it is always yours, it is always with you, if you know that you have it right now, and you will always have it, you will have no attachment to it. Attachment appears when we don't believe we can have something, when we feel lack, frustration, when you don't believe it is ever going to be yours. We feel attached to something when we don't have it, when we are desperate, when we feel the feeling of need. We also get attached to something when we maybe have it, but we are afraid that we might lose it, that something might happen to it, that it will disappear from our life. So, that's again a focus on lack of the desired thing, or possible lack of it in the future. And the reason of why we want it so bad and we like it so much (so desperately), is just because we either don't have it or are afraid of losing it. And that is basically the focus on lack and limitation of that desired thing, because when you have something, you don't want it anymore. You might like it, you might enjoy it, but you are not desperate, you are not needy, you already have it, you are satisfied.

Let's go farther, if you have something, and if you know for million percent, you know for sure, that it is always with you, that nothing bad can ever happen to that thing that you like, that it is always with you, it is always yours, and only better things are awaiting for you in the future, when you know it for sure, there is no attachment to anything anymore.

So, the true nature of attachment is pure lack and limitations, the feeling of lack of that thing, the fear of never getting it, the fear of not getting enough of it or the fear of losing it. And the whole idea of you liking it so much, beyond the "healthy" easy feeling of liking, is also an indicator that shows you that you are focusing on lack, because if you have something, if you know for 1,000,000% that it is yours now and will always be yours, and everything that you will have in the future will only be better than that thing, then you will not want it any more. If you have something, you cannot want it. If you know that it is always with you for sure, you cannot be afraid of losing it or not having enough of it. The whole idea of attachment disappears. That's why it is better not to be attached to anything. It is better not to be attached to any result, because when you are attached you are focusing on lack of that thing that you desire, and guess what you create? More lack.

On the contrary, when you focus on having something you want, when you feel you already have it, when you know for sure that the prayer is already answered, when you trust God, when you are convinced that everything you will have in the future will only be better and better, when you believe and feel that you already have the thing you want, when you are convinced that your prayer is answered, when you have this easy, calm, satisfied, happy feeling filled with love and gratitude, the feeling of the answered prayer, you are focusing your thoughts, your feelings and your beliefs on the thing that you desire. And guess what you create? More of that. You attract what you think, what you focus on, what you feel and what you believe.

Always remember what your true nature is. You are the Divine being, the beloved child of God. Everything you can ever want or need is already here for you. All the riches of the Universe are already here. They are here for you. Always remember about your true goal and the true aspiration of your soul, which is feeling the connection and oneness with the Divine and always moving forward, to God. There will be no attachment whatsoever, if you know and always remember who you really are, what you really have, and what you truly long for.

It is time to transfer your theoretical knowledge on practice. It is time to show with results what you consciously choose, what you choose to believe, what you consciously choose to think and feel. It is your choice and it is the time to see it manifest in reality. It is time to see the results of your knowledge, practice, determination and trust. It is time to choose and live the life of your dreams. The time is now. Say to yourself:

"I am happy, I am healthy, I am wealthy, I am creative, I am beautiful, I am joyous, I am blissful, I am abundant, I am prosperous, I am talented, I am successful. I choose love, gratitude, happiness, good health, wealth, success and joy. I am beloved child of God. I am the perfect creation. I feel the power of the Divine that is in me. I feel love, abundance, joy, success, gratitude and peace of the Divine in me. I trust the Creator. Unconditional, unlimited love of God is always with me. God loves me, He forgives me, He supports me, He takes care of me, He protects me. God is always with me, He is always by my side. I always feel

His unlimited, unconditional love and support. The healing love of God fills my mind, my body and my soul, it fills me completely. I am happy, I am wealthy, I am abundant, I am healthy, I am successful, I am calm, I am peaceful, I am joyous, I am happy."

Say to the Divine:

"Thank You, I love You."

Choose love, choose abundance, choose peace, choose joy, choose success, choose your dreams. Focus on love, focus on wealth, focus on success, focus on happiness. Stay focused on your dreams and goals, stay loyal to them, stay determined. Feel the power of the Divine in you, feel this power. Feel that with His power everything is possible. Trust the Divine in you. Trust God. He always loves you, He takes care of you. His Almighty Power and unconditional Love are always with you. Let go of the result, feel calmness, happiness, thankfulness and satisfaction of the answered prayer. Feel good. Fill yourself with love, gratitude and peace of the Divine. Focus your thoughts and feelings on your dreams and goals, believe and know that you already are the person you want to be. Believe and know to the point of conviction that your prayer is already answered. Believe and know that whatever is perfect and right for you always shows up in your life in the Divine Order. Focus on, think about and feel love, gratitude, success, good health, joy, abundance, wealth, prosperity, bliss, triumph.

Open yourself to the infinite riches and the bountiful gifts of the Universe and know that you are ready to receive them now. You are ready to live the life of your dreams now. You are ready now. You are letting yourself experience the life you dream about and deserve. You are ready and you are opening your doors to the infinite riches of the Universe, to the Divine gifts, that have been waiting for you all along. They have always been here but now you are manifesting them into your life, into your reality. Now is the time for you to choose and reach your goals, and live your dreams. Now you are happy, wealthy, successful, joyous, triumphant and blissful. Feel it, live it, be it. And open yourself to this magnificent beauty of life, open yourself to the infinite riches of the Universe and live the life of your dreams right now. It is already here. Everything already exists in the unlimited, infinite Universe. You just have to believe it, feel it, let yourself have it, trust the Divine, let go of fears, let go of the result and receive it. Just feel the calmness, love, happiness, gratitude and satisfaction of the prayer that has already been answered. It's that easy, it's that genius.

XV

MANIFESTATION FORMULA
AND BEYOND

To sum everything up, we have a formula of manifestation. The first step is to understand what you want and to choose it. Make a clear goal, have a clear vision of this goal, dream, or better to say have a clear feeling of that goal, clear understanding of how you want to feel when you achieve this goal. Understanding of how you want to feel when you achieve your dreams is important, because sometimes, the outcomes are surprising, and the way they come to reality is unpredictable, but they are always perfect when you know the feeling you are looking for.

For example, she wants to marry this guy. She secretly loves him and her desire is to be with him. What might be not such a good idea for her is to say: "My goal is to marry this particular guy." It is much better for her to say: "My goal is to be happy, to find the love of my life, to be with the perfect man for me, to live the life full of love, happiness and understanding with the perfect companion, with my true soul mate." It is more important, in this situation, for this lady to know and to focus on the way she wants to feel when she will get married to the perfect guy for her, than to attach her thoughts to some particular guy, because sometimes we don't know what is perfect and right for us. We might not know everything about the situation. And we don't know about the gifts that are awaiting us in the future. May be tomorrow this lady will meet someone, who is so much better for her, than her today's passion. Maybe, tomorrow, unpredictably, she will meet the true love of her life, someone who will make her happy, who will really love her, and she will really love him. But she does not know about it yet; it still awaits her in the future.

Therefore, it is better to know and to focus on how you want to feel, how you want to feel when your dream will come true. And the Universe will bring the perfect outcome that will match and correspond to your feelings. Sometimes we don't know what is perfect and right for us, we don't know about the beautiful gifts that await us. So, we have to make sure we know how we want to feel when the goal is achieved. We should focus on this feeling, maintain it, and life will open up the perfect possibility that will match your feeling. The Universe will bring you whatever will make you feel that way or even better. And sometimes it can be something different, something new, amazing and different than what we expect, but it will always be something that you have really wanted, but maybe did not know it existed.

So, to come back to our formula of manifestation, first is the understanding of what you want, understanding your dreams and desires, and making a goal. See the clear vision of it, feel the clear feeling of it. And choose it.

Choose to have it. Choose your thoughts, choose your feelings, choose your emotions, choose your reactions. Choose the thoughts, emotions, reactions and feelings that will concentrate on your goal, that will lead you to the achievement of it. And make sure you stay focused on what you want and not on the opposite.

The feelings will help you; they are the indicators of the focus of our thoughts. If you feel good you focus on your desire, if you feel bad you focus on the opposite from what you want, you focus on lack and limitations. So, choose your thoughts. Focus on your goal and stay focused on it. Focus your feelings on your goal and stay focused on it in any situation, no matter what you are suggested by the outside circumstances. Don't let anyone or anything disturb or distract your focus. Don't let the outer world control you, control what is going on inside of you. Make your inner world govern the outer world and manifest what you choose and want.

Always remember that you are the Divine being, the perfect creation, the beloved child of God. There is a part of the Divine in you. There is the Infinite Presence of the Divine in you. There is the power of the Almighty in you. There is the love, wisdom, and abundance of the Divine in you. Always remember that there is only one power that exists, it is the power of the Divine in you. God is the only power that is, and this Power is always with you. God is always with you, He is always by your side. God loves you, protects you, supports you, leads you and takes care of you. His unconditional Love, His boundless Wisdom, and His

Almighty Power are always with you. *"For God all things are possible."* (Matthew 19:26)

So, let's repeat it again, understand what you want, understand how you want to feel, make a goal and choose it. Choose the thoughts, feelings, emotions and reactions that will focus on and correspond to your goal. Educate yourself, study the laws of the Universe, improve yourself and get rid of the negative false beliefs and of prejudices, superstitions, fads, and fear that these false beliefs bring with them. Trust and rely on the Only Power that exists — God. Feel the Love and Power of God inside of you; feel His infinite, unconditional Love and His Almighty Power, which are always with you.

Feel good. Get rid of self-criticism and any judgment towards others. Get rid of feelings that make no sense, bring no good and poison our life. These feelings are guilt, anger, resentment, hate, jealousy, greed, self-condemnation. Forgive yourself and forgive others. The past is long time gone. Free yourself from it. It does not exist anymore. These negative feelings don't help you. There is no sense in feeling something that does not exist anymore and something that does not do any good to you.

Let go of all negativity. What we feel we attract, we follow our vision. What we feel and think about, what we focus on we bring into our reality. Fill yourself with love and gratitude. Become a part of this endless ocean of the Divine Love of the Universe and let it heal your wounds. Let the love of the Divine fill your soul, your mind and your body. Feel it, live it, be it. Fill yourself with calmness, peace, happiness and joy of the Divine. Align with the endless, unlimited love, peace, prosperity, gratitude and joy of the Universe.

Affirmations, mediations and repetition of the Divine Truths help to align with the positive rhythm of life. If you remain focused on the things that are good, things that are godlike, things that are true, on love, happiness, bliss, wealth, abundance and joy, if you keep on practicing techniques that help you stay focused on the positive things you've chosen, these positive things and ideas eventually sink into your subconsciousness. You repeat them over and over again and they become your inner beliefs, a part of your nature, they become natural and automatic to you, they become your truth, your convictions. When your conscious mind, your conscious desire, your goals, agree with your subconsciousness, your feelings, your inner beliefs, your convictions, and your inner beliefs deeply seated in your heart, then your goals manifest into reality, they show up on the surface of your reality.

Everything already exists in the infinite possibilities of the Universe. All we have to do is to allow ourselves to have what we want, to open up to the infinite riches that are here, that have always been waiting for us. If we are open, if we are ready, if our mind is ready, if our inner state is ready, if we are aligned with and if we are in this positive, loving, abundant rhythm of the Universe, everything just happens. When you are ready, things just happen, the life prepares every little circumstance, it puts them in the right order, in the perfect sequence for the best outcomes, for the outcomes that are far beyond anything we've ever wanted, and it happens with ease. It happens easy. It happens on its own. All you have to do is to receive it.

Let's repeat it one more time, understand what you want and how you want to feel. Make a goal, have a dream, choose it. Choose your thoughts, feelings, emotions and reactions. Stay focused on your goal; see it with your inner vision. Feel your inner worth. You deserve all the best in life. You are the Divine being. You are perfect, you are amazing, you are beautiful, you are talented. You are the beloved child of God. Make yourself ready, make your mind and your feelings ready. Your goal and your higher vision of yourself are deeply seated in your inner beliefs; they are your truth now. You are convinced that you are a winner, that success, wealth, and triumph are yours. This is felt and seen in each of your move, in each of your step, in each of your word, in each of your thought, in each of your action. You consciously choose your inner beliefs. They sink into your subconsciousness, becoming your truth, and this truth governs your actions and leads you to your goals.

And trust, trust the Divine in you. Trust God. And with this trust comes peace and calmness. There is no need or desire to control the situation. There is no feeling of desperation, of want or need. Let the human, your ego, relax and let the Divine inspiration work miracles in your life. The feeling of ease, freedom, peace, calmness and love fills you. This feeling of ease and freedom feels like you don't even have to do anything physical to bring about that goal. And maybe, you really would not have to do anything, sometimes the desired outcome just happens, when you are ready. And even if you would have to do something, it would feel so easy, so joyous, so natural, that it would feel like you are just following your heart and that everything is happening on its own.

Don't get me wrong — sometimes we all have to work a lot and very hard in order to achieve something. We have to work on ourselves, educate and improve ourselves, study the laws of the Universe, and work hard at work or build the business, and do things that need to be done. Very often we have to go out of our comfort zone. But if you know that you always win, if you believe in your success, if your inner truth is that you are successful, wealthy and triumphant, if you see the clear vision of who you want to be, what you want to achieve, and how you want to feel; if you align with the Divine Truths of the Universe; if you feel your connection with the Only Power that exists, God; if you feel your oneness with the Divine; then you are inspired to the perfect and right actions. Your talents spring and you live in the constant glory of the life that expresses itself through you. You open yourself to your fullest potential, you are led through the perfect path to whatever is perfect for you, to whatever is best for you, to whatever is right for you. And you become the person you want to be, because you already are that person. You just have to believe it, feel it, let yourself be that person, open yourself to the Divine Love and inspiration, which will heal and transform all the aspects of your life to whatever is perfect and right for you.

Let's repeat it again, understand what you want, how you want to feel and make a goal. Chose it, choose your thoughts, feelings and reactions. Focus on your goal. Make your consciousness (your mind) and your subconsciousness (your feelings, your inner beliefs) agree on your desire. Make yourself ready. Change your inner beliefs to positive ones, to beliefs that are true and that serve you. Change the perception of yourself and of your life to the positive one, to the one that is true, and that serves you and humanity. Fill yourself with trust to the Divine, with love and goodwill. Be in the good mood, feel good. Believe, know, be convinced and feel that you already are the person you want to be and that you already have what you want.

Know that everything already exists in the infinite possibilities of the Universe. You just have to feel it, believe it, believe that you have it. Believe and feel that you have already reached your goal, that you are at the top of your triumph. You've worked so hard. You've worked on yourself, you've disciplined your thoughts, your feelings, your reactions to outer things and circumstances. So much work has already been done. Now you can relax and rejoice. Enjoy your achievements, enjoy your success, welcome your triumph and open your door to the riches that are here. They have always been here; they have always been here for you.

Celebrate your triumph, anticipate and foretaste your awards, the gifts. At the same time, feel calm, peaceful, feel free. Relax, let go of the result, let go of any excessive want, need, desperation. Let go of the situation. Let go of the outcome. Feel love, gratitude, calmness, ease, satisfaction and happiness of the answered prayer. Calm down any excessive excitement. Relax, and enjoy this moment, this second. Enjoy your life, enjoy the process. Be certain that your goal is already here. Feel that you already reached your goal. Be calm, satisfied and happy. Rejoice at the things you've already achieved, and calmly but surely foretaste the rewards, feeling that they are already here. You already are the person you want to be. You already have all the riches of the Universe. They have always been here, but now you are open to them, you believe you have them, you feel them, you are ready and you are receiving your dreams. Feel it now and the results will not make you wait for long.

Feel this grateful calmness. Feel gratitude and love towards everything that exists, towards yourself, towards the world, towards the Divine, towards everything you have already done and achieved. That's the right spirit! There is a good fellow! You did it! Feel the feelings of success, worthiness, love and pride. Be proud of yourself. Feel this amazing calmness, joy, relaxation, ease, freedom, happiness and bliss on the peak of your triumph! Feel it! It feels so good! It tastes so good! This moment is perfect; and your future, your entire existence, is amazing, is divinely perfect!

So, if you feel this way, if you feel your success, if you feel the way you want to feel, if you feel that you are the person you want to be, if you feel that your goal is already here, that it is already achieved, and at the same time you trust the Divine, you feel oneness with the Divine, everything else just follows. If you let go of the result, and feel ease, freedom and joy, if you are calm, peaceful, relaxed, happy and satisfied (like you are everything you've ever wanted to be and you have everything you've ever wanted to have) and you enjoy this moment (as if it cannot be more perfect than it is), everything just happens. It happens on its own, because you are ready, because you are open to it, because you are aligned with it! Like attracts like, and now you are doing it.

We have to stay strong and be persistent. When you find your goal, when you feel good, when you feel oneness with the Divine, do not let anything distract or disturb you. Be strong in yourself, be determined. And protect yourself from anything negative that surrounds you. Don't let it inside of you. Sometimes we cannot run away from our surroundings, and from the information we receive from the outside. Therefore we have to develop a strong protection, become immune (inside) towards this information. Many things that disturb our inner peace are not even real, like fads, strange thoughts, prejudices, superstitions, some kinds of fear of unknown. Very often these things are just a product of our imagination that is channeled in the wrong direction. For example, we hear something on the news, we read about something, or our friend tells us about something, or sometimes people pick up negative information even without noticing it, and then they suffer from negative thoughts that bother them inside, and disturb their peace. So we have to be strong in ourselves, stay loyal to the truths that we have chosen, to the Divine Truths, and we have to become immune to anything else.

The outer is someone else's perception. Don't allow someone else's perceptions of life or of the events and circumstances poison your inner feelings and govern your life. Everything that makes us feel bad is the outer, someone else's perception, and it is a false perception, because what is real, what is true, feels good, and is in tune with the natural harmony that is inside of us. It is our nature, it is natural to us. We can judge inside of us what is good and what is bad, because good is natural to us, because something within us reminds us of our origin. Something within you tells you what is natural to you and it calls you back, it calls you to the Source, which is love, harmony, beauty, and peace.

Don't let someone's false, negative perceptions of the world influence you. Choose your own true perceptions, which are based on the Divine Truths. And you will feel deep within you that it is truth and that it is your nature, because it will feel natural to you, it will feel like you.

When you feel bad, it is an indicator that something unnatural to you, something foreign to you, is trying to get close to you; and your entire being is resisting, cannot and does not want to accept it, to be with it, to take it in. That's why it feels bad. It is not yours. It is not you. It is not your true nature, and it is false. Why do we even need to bother with it then? Choose the Divine Truth, be with it, feel it, live it, be it. Choose your true Divine nature. Choose your own true perceptions of life, which are based on the Divine Truths, on the laws of the Universe. Choose what is natural to you. Choose what is the true nature of your origin, what is really you. The understanding of this, together with your constant self-improvement, and maintaining of the feeling of oneness with the Divine is the strongest protection ever from the false, needless, painful, negative, outside, someone else's perceptions and ideas, from bad feelings, non-acquaintance and fear.

Free yourself from anything that is not you, choose and fill yourself with the Divine Truths, love and inspiration, feel oneness with God, and you will feel this endless unlimited constant connection to the Source, and you will be and you will feel what you really long for deep in your heart.

Always fill yourself with the Divine Truths. Don't even give a slight chance for anything else to come even close to you, to your inner world! Self-educate yourself, learn the laws of the Universe, meditate, fill yourself with the Divine Truths, with love, gratitude, happiness, health, wealth, joy, abundance, goodwill, bliss, success and triumph. Always feed your brain with positive godlike ideas. Nothing stays the same; nothing stays constant in this Universe. If you don't choose and fill yourself with the Divine Truths, something else will fill the "empty" space, and that "something else" might not be always pleasant, or something that will make you feel good or serve you. Therefore, always make your choice for yourself. Deep in your heart you know what to choose, because it is you, and it calls you. So follow your heart. Fill yourself with love, happiness, bliss, triumph, joy, gratitude, good health, beauty, peace and harmony. Feel your connection to the Divine, feel oneness with God. Feel good. Feel the love, the harmony, the peace, and the happiness of God within you, and you will always find your true place, you will always have whatever is perfect and right for you in the Divine Order.

We often tend to work on ourselves the hardest when we are at our downside. When something happens, when we are hurt, when we feel pain, we start acting in order to eliminate that pain; and it is good. Remember, we are always guided by the Divine and often some things that might look bad or undesirable at first, are simply leading us to where we are supposed to go, to our goals. Our inner natural aspiration is always to better, to positive, to good, to the higher levels of our existence in everything (in every aspect of our life), always forward, always to where you belong, to God. And when we are sent something that we consider not a desirable outcome, when we feel bad, or when something happens not the way we want, very often these situations and feelings just show us that we need to improve ourselves, educate ourselves, let go of something, act and start our quest for what we are looking for. These situations, very often, push us towards self-growth, self-improvement and towards our achievements. They kind of show you: "Oh, you don't want to go this way, you don't like this experience, you don't like this feeling, you don't like to be poor, you don't like to feel pain, you don't like to be lonely. Good!" Now you can choose what you like, improve yourself, grow, understand and come to what your soul is truly aiming for, and achieve your goals.

So, we often tend to work harder on ourselves when we feel worse or when we feel bad, and we do this in order to improve our situation or state; and, as we discussed earlier, it is good. But wouldn't it be better to work the best on ourselves, when we are at our best, when we feel the best? What happens very often is that when we feel bad we start to work hard, we try to grow mentally, spiritually, but as soon as we feel better, or feel good, or maybe even reach our goals and dreams, we kind of stop, or slow down our self-growth process. At this point we just try to enjoy our achievements. This is great, amazing, but try to be careful not to slide down to the passive mode. Remember, nothing is constant. If you don't fill yourself with Divine Truths and things that you like, and choose, if you don't feed your brain with the Divine principles of life, if you don't fill your heart with love, peace, calmness and wisdom of God, and if you don't maintain it, the passive "empty" space will be taken by something else, by somebody else's thoughts, feelings and suggestions. And what comes from the outside and from the mass mind might not be what you want, what you choose and what serves you.

When people start feeling bad again, only then they remind themselves: "Oh, I haven't meditated for a while," or "maybe I should read this book." Or "where are my affirmations?" And they try to work on themselves again, which is great. But it is really amazing to keep this feeling of love, happiness, peace, success and bliss all the time, to nourish it, to maintain it. It is important to always grow, always move forward, to God. Therefore, follow the true call of your heart and soul all the time. Grow and improve yourself. Feel oneness with the Divine. Fill yourself with the Divine Truths, love, peace, happiness, health, wealth, joy, bliss, success, godlike thoughts and ideas. Always feel the Divine Love, gratitude and peace in your heart.

Change your attitude, change your mentality, change your approach to this process. Working on yourself, improving yourself and growing when you feel bad, in order to make the situation better is good, but working on yourself, improving and growing when you feel the best, because you want to feel even better is amazing. Plus, imagine how effective it can be to always maintain harmony, peace, love, gratitude, bliss and happiness in your heart, rather than just try to always bring yourself back to the position of stability after a great emotional fall; and again it is pretty good, too. It does not matter how you grow and improve yourself, as long as you do it. But it can be easier, more efficient, more pleasant, and maybe even faster and on a deeper level, if you always maintain this feeling of inner connection with the Divine, the oneness with God, love, peace, gratitude, harmony, success, abundance, bliss and happiness in your heart, in your soul, if you maintain it, keep it, grow it, always moving forward to God. Imagine how different everything will be, if you always feel good, easy, happy, healthy, wealthy, abundant, successful, blissful, if you always feel love, peace, gratitude, harmony and happiness in your heart and your soul, if your thoughts are always filled with the Divine Truths. When you feel connection and oneness with the Divine, your life becomes an endless miracle of God, because it really is so, but now you can feel it.

There is something beyond all knowledge, all the rules, all the education, more than anything you can do, think or feel, more than any plan or dream or desire, more than anything you can practice. It's the being, the Living Presence of God in everything that exists. It is the only truth, the only thing you can be sure of, the only thing you can trust and know for sure.

In the instances when everything you know fails, the theories, practices and beliefs don't work, you can always turn to the Divine Presence that always is, to this endless, infinite Presence of everything that is and that isn't. It is beyond any thought or feeling, or action. It is beyond any knowledge or explanation. It is beyond any experience. It is throughout everything that is and that isn't. It is everything that is and everything that isn't. It is endless, unlimited, unconditional, infinite being, calm, peaceful, loving Presence of the eternity. It was never born, it cannot die, it always is. It cannot be labeled. It cannot be put in any frames or restraints. It is limitless, it is boundless, it is beyond anything our present understanding can grasp. It is everything that is and everything that is not, everything that will ever be and everything that will ever be not, because everything that is and everything that is not, is everything that is and everything that will ever be, the limitless, endless, boundless, unconditional, unlimited Presence, the breath of the existence, the love of the eternity, the movement of the infinity. The endless, unlimited, loving Presence of God that is in you, in me, in every one of us and in everything that is.

Therefore, if all you know fails, if the knowledge, the theories, and practices do not help, you always have something that is beyond any knowledge, any practice or theory, something you can always trust and come to, something that always has the answers, something that is always with you, something that is everything you'll ever need, it is the loving Presence of God within you and within everything that is. Tune yourself with the Divine Truths of the God Presence. Think about it, feel it, meditate with it. Feel your connection and oneness with the Divine. Dissolve in the love and freedom of God. Feel oneness with this endless, unlimited, unconditional, infinite, boundless ocean of love of the Divine.

We might not always know what is best for ourselves; after all, we don't know what will happen next. Sometimes we don't even know what we want. We are clueless of what will happen. At times we don't know what is that we really want and need. That's what we chose to experience here in our earthly life. We pretended to forget our origin and we are called to look for it, that's why we are here, it is a part of the genius "game" we've chosen to experience. The only thing we can know for sure is that God is all that is, and that He is always with you, He is always by your side. Align with the Divine Truths, tune in with godlike thoughts, feelings and ideas. Let go of everything else. Feel your connection, your oneness with God. He brings whatever is perfect and right for you. Let go of the result completely. Let go of any want, or need, or desperation.

Don't try to align with the Divine Truths in order to get something. Align with the godlike ideas, because it is the true call of your soul, and it is. Trust the Divine, and everything else will just follow, it will happen on its own. Put God first, and everything that is perfect and everything that is right for you will just follow with ease. It will happen naturally, on its own. The Divine inspiration will govern your life. The Divine Wisdom and Truth will lead you. The Divine Love will fill you, your inner world, your mind, your body, your soul. And the right actions will follow, and perfect results will manifest, when you are ready.

God is always with you anyways. He always leads you, no matter if you are in tune with the Divine Truths or not, because you are always the Divine being, no matter if you are aware of or realize your true nature or not. You are the Divine being; you are the beloved child of God. So, God is always by your side. He is always with you. He always leads you, loves you and protects you. He always shows you the way. God always sends you the inspiration, the wisdom, the answers, but we are not always ready to hear them. We are not always open to them. We are not always in tune with them.

We block the inspiration, we are filled with fears, negativity, wrong beliefs and false prejudices suggested form the outside. We are not clear. We don't feel, don't hear, don't allow, don't accept the beauty, the love, the wealth, the success and the bliss of this life. These gifts, these blessings are always here, they are always here for you. Just open yourself to them. Open yourself to God, to His love, to His inspiration. Open yourself to the bountiful, unlimited, boundless riches of the Universe which are all around you, which are all for you. Feel the oneness with the Divine and live the life of the beloved child of God, because you are the beloved child of God. You just have to see it, realize it, believe it, allow yourself to be who you truly are, open yourself to God, and accept all the love, beauty and riches that are beyond any imagination possible. These riches are beyond anything you've ever seen or experienced, because they are gifts of God to His beloved child. They are the manifestations of the Creator for Himself, because we are parts of the Whole. The part of the Divine is in us, in each and every one of us. And when we are open, when we are ready, we live the life of the paradise here on earth.

And this is the life of balance. The Divine Love, inspiration, right actions and perfect results show up in every aspect of your life. The balance and harmony of the Divine dwell in you and in every part of your existence. The love of God fills and heals your finances, your personal life, your relationships with everyone around you, your physical state and condition, your family, your business, your health. It fulfills your spiritual quest, it stabilizes and harmonizes your emotional wellbeing. The Divine inspiration leads you to the right actions and the right choices, and only everything that is perfect, everything that is right for you, shows up in all aspects of your life. And you live the life of the balanced happiness, wealth and abundance, balanced and harmonious triumph, success and bliss. You become complete and whole, because when you are with God, you are complete, you are whole. Your dreams fulfill, because they are the dreams of God. He has sent them to you. His Presence is in you. His awareness is in you and it is expressed through your thoughts and feelings. There is a power of the Divine in you and you direct it through your thoughts and feelings. So, God Himself manifests whatever is perfect and whatever is right for you, into your reality. And there is a perfect balance, peace, love, happiness, health, wealth, triumph, success, bliss, joy and harmony in every aspect of your existence.

Deep inside we all know our true and main aim in life. All your being longs for it, even if you don't realize it on your conscious level yet. Everything in you calls to your true origin. The deepest thirst of your soul is the thirst for Divine Truths and oneness with God. We are here to express our fullest potential, because the Divine Presence expresses itself through us. And our biggest aim is to always move forward, to God. Trust Him with all your heart, with all your soul, with all your inner feelings, with all your existence. Trust and love God with all your heart.

Feel this inner harmony, peace, satisfaction, calmness, bliss, joy and happiness. Feel gratitude and love for God. Feel the trust and love to God with all your heart, with all your soul, with all your being. It is indescribable by words; you just have to feel it.

Everything comes and goes, everything changes, but God is always with you. His Presence is always in you. God is always with you. He is your foundation, your savior, everything you will ever need. And He is always with you. He is always by your side. His love, protection, support, peace, power, care and endless, unconditional love are always with you. God is always with you. He is always by your side. Realize it, know it, feel it. Feel the trust, gratitude and love to God deep in your heart and your soul. Feel peace, calmness, harmony, happiness, abundance and bliss of the Divine in your heart. Feel the trust, gratitude and love to God deep in your heart, in your soul, in all your being.

Love this life, love yourself and the world around you, love everything that is. Love God. Be thankful, harmonious and peaceful. Fill yourself with love and gratitude, calmness and peace of the Divine. Feel the oneness with God. And live the amazing balanced life full of happiness, miracles, wealth, triumph, abundance, bliss and success!

God be with you!
Zoey Zlatoslava

Zoey Zlatoslava Petrak

XVI

CONCLUSION

FOR YOU

For you the whole world is created
And don't say anything right now,
With you, the dawn and the twilight,
The forests, fields and seas.
Don't leave them all behind.

The heartbeat of the wind, the breath of stars,
The noise of rain are yours forever and again.
The world's hope and the light,
The Earth spins and sings for you and it is all Divine.

You create and you are the creation.
You are loved and you are love yourself.
You are the eternity's heartbeat and its vibration,
You are the flesh and blood of life itself.

When you are along – you are not lonely,
The whole world is by your side.
When you are down – you are high and only,
Observe intentions of your chosen ride.

Look at the sky
With blue or gray, or rose clouds,
It is all created just for you.
You are in caring hands,
With love, be proud.
And know that He is always here for you.

In the embrace of snow,
In drops of breezy rain,
The child is always safe
In the sun's beautiful and caring rays.

Look, redolent fields,
The tweet of birds, the forest stream,
The ocean's powerful smooth surface,
Crags and mountains,
Look from their high shoulders straight beneath.

You will see the life's conceiving,
Infant's laughter, endless wisdom of the gray haired men.
You will understand the bliss, and inspiration,
You will feel fulfillment of your most delightful dreams.

BIBLIOGRAPHY

1. *Holy Bible.* Nashville: Thomas Nelson, Inc., 1989.